Puppet Scripts for Use at Church

Selected and Edited by Everett Robertson

BROADMAN PRESS
Nashville, Tennessee

Contents

Introduction

Puppetry has historically been an important means of communication. The inanimate object suddenly springing to life with human characteristics has long fascinated men. This fascination permits puppets to communicate the realities of human experience in a manner often impossible in other communicative media.

Records indicate that medieval churches used puppets in their services, and we know that early civilizations incorporated them in their rituals. In recent years many Southern Baptist churches have used puppets throughout their ministry with great success. The rapid growth of the puppet ministry has established an urgent need for church-oriented puppet materials. This collection of published and unpublished materials is intended to fill part of that need and to provide guidance for development of additional materials by performing groups.

A variety of puppets and script materials are potentially useful to the church. This collection does not limit itself to a specific style of puppet or puppet script. In fact, some of the scripts simply call for two or more puppets of any style.

The intent has been to make the scripts as flexible as possible. Editorial comment within the framework of individual scripts has been limited where possible. The puppeteer is free to use his imagination in interpreting character and subject matter. Ideally, no individual script will need to be produced exactly the same way by any two groups. The scripts may be used as an outline for development of other scripts of similar length and style.

Scenic requirements and other technical equipment for most of the scripts is minimal. Each puppet team can utilize existing resources to support the scripts with technical materials. Lighting, for example, may or may not be used. Some of the longer scripts offer many opportunities to use extensive technical equipment and materials if these are available.

Certain characters reappear in some scripts throughout the collection. These characters have evolved through years of production experience by the writers. You may wish to select certain puppet characters to reappear in your productions.

The scripts are listed under five general categories or sections. Some scripts may fit in several categories, but all are listed under one of five headings. The "Fun and Fellowship" section has fewer scripts because many scripts in other categories may also be used in this area.

The scripts vary greatly in length and form. Some require only puppets. Others use teachers, actors, or planned responses by members of the audience.

Many of the scripts are designed for youth or adults and are inappropriate for children. The children's worker will need to take care in selecting scripts to be used in Sunday School or Church Training. The scripts should be selected based on philosophy presented in *Getting Ready for Children's Sunday School Work* and *Teaching Children in Sunday School*. Both of these books are available in Baptist Book Stores. They are published by Convention Press.

The collection is intended primarily for the performing puppeteer. But, the fascination of puppets and the variety of scripts make this an excellent collection to read just for fun.

The cassette tape which accompanies this collection contains selected scripts. If the tape is used, the puppets pantomime with the voices on the tape.

This collection directly supports the book *Using Puppetry in the Church*. The techniques necessary for using these scripts in the puppet ministry are presented in that book. Major areas of the book include: When and where to use puppets in the church, handling and manipulating puppets, teaching with puppets, rehearsal and production techniques, decorating and costuming puppets, scenery and props for puppets, lighting and sound, puppet patterns of varying types and sizes, and patterns for puppet stages. Some other areas covered in the book are: Writing puppet scripts, touring with puppets, developing puppet character, and using marionettes.

Using Puppetry in the Church contains the basic techniques for developing and continuing a total puppet ministry. The book is available in Baptist Book Stores. For additional information on puppetry contact the Church Recreation Department, Baptist Sunday School Board, 127 Ninth Avenue North, Nashville, Tennessee 37234.

Section I

PROMOTION
WITH PUPPETS

Use Us!*

by Rob Williams

Sally, Grandma, Tom

(Sally and Grandma enter. A boy hurries by, as though trying to get to a seat before the show starts. Sally leans far over the stage, watching him with wonder.)

Sally: Grandma, what was that?

Grandma: *(Pointing)* That? Oh, that's a person.

Sally: A person? What's that?

Grandma: Oh, people are very complex creatures. Why, they sometimes do things just because they've always done them—or they don't do things because they're new and different. They are what control us, you know.

Sally: *(Looks down)* Oh, them?

Grandma: Yes. *(Tom enters)*

Tom: *(Over-dramatically)* "Oh, that this too, too solid flesh would melt, thaw, and resolve itself into a dew. . ."

Sally: *(Holding her ears)* Stop! Please stop!

Tom: You don't know good acting when you see it. Well, okay; I can't help it if you have no taste. *(Dejected, he bends his head, and then suddenly changes his tone.)* Grandma, why are we here?

Grandma: What do you mean, Tom?

Tom: I mean, what are puppets for? Why do they make us?

Grandma: Well, because it's fun. Why, you were made in a Bible School, and Sally was made in a crafts class, and. . .

Tom: But why? What do they do with us after they make us?

Sally: Oh, I know that. They . . . they . . . They put us on a shelf in the closet and forget us. *(Mildly angry)* They don't know how it feels. *(Pointing an accusing finger to someone in the audience)* Have you ever had a spider build his web on your face? It's not very funny! *(To Grandma)* They don't use us.

Grandma: Oh, but they do now. I remember when I was just a piece of cloth. . .

Tom: Oh, here it goes.

Grandma: Mind your elders! As I was saying, I was so excited to be made. They played with me for a while, but then it wore off. I never got to go anywhere very often, and then only to children's departments.

Sally: Don't you like children, Grandma?

Grandma: Oh, goodness yes, Sally. I love children. But I do like a bit of adult company now and then. Why, you young puppets are lucky. They're beginning to use you more.

Tom: Yes, but they still don't use us enough.

Grandma: Well, you have to understand them, dear. People are like puppets in some ways—they are all controlled by something.

Sally: By what?

Grandma: The wise ones are controlled by God. With the others, it is many things. Often they are controlled by blind tradition. Those are the ones who think that anything but preaching in church is wrong.

Sally: But I thought the idea of church was to spread the gospel—in whatever way is effective.

Grandma: It is, but as I said, you have to understand them.

Tom: I don't care what their excuse is. I want to do my part in church. I'm not limited; I can do things. I can witness, and to all ages—from preschoolers to adults. I want to get out and work. I want to help tell people about Christ.

Sally: So do I. If I didn't have to depend on people to control me, I'd be out witnessing every day—in Bible School, in day camp, in Sunday School, on mission trips, on retreats, on street corners, in Church Training, and even in worship services.

Grandma: *(Gasps)* In worship services? Don't let an adult person hear you say that!

Tom: How can we get through to people, Grandma? How can we convince them to use us to our full ability—for teaching, for humor, for witnessing . . . How can we tell them?

Sally: I know! *(Pause)* We can give a puppet show. . .

The September Rush*

by Tom deGraaf

Willie, Sally, Cool Charlie, Sammy Schmulker

Willie: Well, here it is—Back to school time again. Old bum-trip school. Dad says he's glad summer's over so he can send us kids back to someone who can handle us!

Sally: *(Enters)* Oh. Hi! Willie. What'cha thinkin' about?

Willie: I gotta go back to school. I can't stand it!

Sally: What are you gripping about? Considering you, I'm sure the school is even more irked at the prospect. You're the dumbest student they've ever had or heard of.

Willie: *(Indignant)* I resent that! Ask me a question—anything! I can answer it—go ahead—ask me!

Sally: OK, William Buckley, name one animal that is extinct!

Willie: Our hamster! The cat extincted him this morning! A Haw Haw Haw!

Sally: *(Creams him)* Now shut up a minute, Einstein! We got a real problem to discuss, and it's more important than your assault on higher education!

Willie: *(Sobers)* What's the problem Golden Gloves?

Sally: The problem is that since school is starting again, we're going to have a whole bunch of new kids coming to our church.

Willie: So what's the problem? I don't understand.

Sally: Well, if we don't have some way to interest our September rush of kids, we'll probably have an October rash of dropouts. We've got to come up with something for these kids to get involved in. Now, have I made myself plain? Have I made myself plain?!!

Willie: If you haven't, nature certainly has! Haw Haw.

Charlie: *(Enters)* Hey Baby! What's so funny?

Sally: Oh, Willie thinks he's some sort of wit. Somebody ought to tell him his name isn't in "Who's Who," but his picture is in "What's This?"

Charlie: Sally, Baby! I've hardly ever seen you this summer! I guess I will, now that school has started and vacations are over! I'll be comin' back to church and seein' everybody!

Sally: Cool Charlie, that's our problem.

Charlie: That's cold Sally. That's really the chills.

Sally: I didn't mean it that way Cool Charlie. What I meant was how are we going to involve our September rush of new kids?

Charlie: Hmmmm . . . I see your meaning. . .

Willie: Why don't we sponsor an all-church football game? We could have the youth play the deacons and the winner of that game meets the W.M.U in the "Judgement Bowl!" *(Laughs)*

Sally: *(Irritated)* Why don't we sponsor a sequel to *Jaws* and cast you as bait? Now get serious Willie! We've got a problem to solve!

Sam: *(Enters timidly; is shy, nervous)* Oh, hi everybody.

Charlie: Hey, it's Sammy Schmulker! What's happening?

Willie: Hi Sammy! How was summer?

Sam: Rotten—I had acne the whole time.

Sally: Sammy, never mind these guys. You've got to help me with a problem. We've got fifty million new kids coming into church right now. How are we going to get them involved in some sort of worthwhile project here at church?

Sam: That's simple. . .

All: It is?

Sam: Sure. All of you look behind this stage. *(They all look)* Now, What do you see??

Sally: Some dummies holding on to the other end of us!

Sam: That's it! We'll get some of these new kids involved in the Puppet Ministry!

Willie: Out-a-sight!

Charlie: Brilliant idea Schmulker! Brilliant!

Sally: Well, if these dummies can do it, I'll bet those dummies out there *(audience)* can do it!

Sam: Sure they can! And I'll help them get started!

Sally: Well that sure puts my mind at ease! Now our new youth will have something fun and meaningful to do!

Charlie: Right on Sally Baby! Now let's us zip over to the library and look at a few *National Geographics*! It's study time. *(They start to exit. Sally and Willie stop)*

Sally: How come since school's started all the other kids have had lots of homework and you never have any?

Willie: Easy. I've adjusted myself to *inferior* grades. *(They exit)*

Vacation Bible School Skit

by Joan King

Sammy, Bernie, Jimmy, Sally

Sammy: Hey, Bernie, what are you doing?

Bernie: Stretching my mouth.

Sammy: Stretching your mouth? Bernie, why would anybody want to stretch his mouth?

Bernie: To make it wider of course!

Jimmy: Well, why do you want to make it wider?

Bernie: The Bible says to. Psalm 81:10 says, "Open thy mouth wide and I will fill it." I'm only trying to apply the Bible to my everyday life!

Sally: That's silly, Bernie. The Bible doesn't mean for you to stretch your mouth. You've missed the point of the Bible verse, Bernie.

Bernie: How do you know what the Bible means? By what authority do you tell me that the Bible doesn't mean for me to stretch my mouth?

Jimmy: Sally means that the Bible teaches us different lessons in many different ways. Sometimes we have to examine Bible stories deeply to understand their true meanings.

Sammy: Bernie, why don't you attend Vacation Bible School with us? Maybe you will discover some new truths about the Bible to apply to your everyday life.

Bernie: OK. Tell me all about it.

Sammy: It is going to be held at _____ Baptist Church, __(date)__ from _____ to _____ . Teen time is at night from _____ to _____ .

Get in the Car, Ralph*

by Don Blackley

Mama, Ralph, Shawn

Mama: *(Hurrying on stage)* Hurry, Ralph! We don't want to be late for Bible School on the very first day.

Ralph: *(Offstage)* Hey, Mama. Remember that Captain Crunch cereal I spilled at breakfast?

Mama: Yes, Son, don't step on it.

Ralph: Mama, how do you get Captain Crunch off the bottom of your shoes?

Mama: Oh, Son, just drag your feet on the carpet and let's go! *(Ralph enters)* Now jump in the car. They're probably lining up outside the door already. *(Shawn enters)*

Shawn: Hi, Ralph. Let's go see if we can find enough guys to play some softball.

Ralph: I can't now Shawn. I'm going to Vacation Bible School up at church.

Mama: *(Impatiently)* Come on and get in the car, Ralph.

Shawn: Vacation Bible School? What do you do there?

Mama: Let's go, Ralph.

Ralph: We have stories, and sing, and make neat things. But the best part is we get refreshments every day!

Mama: *(Exasperated)* It's time Ralph!

Shawn: Refreshments? Wow, can I go?

Ralph: Sure you can. You can ride with us. Can't he Mama? Can't he? Can't he?

Mama: Well, I suppose so, but you'd better run and ask your mother first.

Shawn: Cool! Be back in a minute. *(Runs offstage)*

Mama: Ralph, I'm sorry that I kept rushing you while you were inviting Shawn to Bible School. Now that I think about it, maybe taking someone with us is more important than being on time.

Ralph: Yeah. Remember when the pastor asked everybody to be a V.B.S. bus driver for their neighborhood? Today when I get home I can go ask Sally and Richard and Arnold and Harriet and Clarence and . . .

Mama: Get in the car, Ralph! *(Characters exit)*

Keeping Up-to-Date

by Sarah Walton Miller

Three Puppets

One: You're going with us to the Bible study, aren't you?

Two: *(Eagerly)* Sure he is! We always do things together.

Three: Not this time.

Two: What?

Three: I'm not going.

One: Why not? Have we done something wrong?

Three: No, it's not that.

Two: Then what is it?

Three: Oh—I don't want to hurt your feelings.

Two: *(Puzzled)* Feelings?

Three: Yeah. You two are so set on going to this Bible study. I'm just as set on not going.

One: *(Insisting)* Why?

Three: Oh, because.

One: That's no reason. There has to be a real reason.

Two: You might as well tell us.

Three: Okay, you asked for it. I don't happen to think the Bible means much any more.

Two: *(Shocked)* What?

Three: Not today. Maybe a long time ago. Things are different now. All those old stories—well, they don't mean much anymore.

Two: *(Shocked)* I'm surprised at you!

Three: Well, you asked me!

One: I suppose you think, for instance, the newspaper teaches you more than the Bible, huh?

Three: At least it's true and it's current.

Two: The Bible is true!

Three: And long out-of-date.

One: *(Picks up little newspaper)* Well, let's just see what the newspaper says and what we can learn that's up-to-date. Here's a headline: "Government Directs Building of New Religion Center." Of course you couldn't find that in the Bible.

Three: That's my point—although I don't quite approve of the government getting into religion.

Two: A little religion wouldn't hurt 'em!

Three: If it's for all religions, I guess it's okay.

Two: Where is it to be?

One: It's already *been*. Several thousand years ago. You'll find it in 2 Chronicles 2, where Solomon built the Temple.

Three: That's not fair! You're faking it!

One: Just telling the truth! The Bible is full of headline stories. You couldn't tell if one was from the Bible or the newspaper.

Three: Try me!

One: What about this heading: "Garden Infested with Snakes."

Three: Probably in a new suburb. you always have to fight pests when you build on new land.

Two: That's so.

One: Wrong. Look in Genesis 3 about the Garden of Eden.

Two: Oh, I get it! Read us another one.

One: All right. "Man Survives Attack by Huge Fish."

Three: Sharks! That's it! The sharks that wounded several swimmers!

One: Wrong again. Look in the Bible at Jonah 1 and 2.

Two: *(Gleefully)* I like this!

One: Here's one: "Strange Phenomenon Saves Nomads From Starving."

Three: Is that about our wheat or corn crop?

Two: I get it! That's the *manna* God sent to the Israelites!

One: Right. From Exodus 16. What about this one: "Itinerant Preacher Rescues Woman from Mob."

Three: That *has* to be a real headline. Probably in Bangkok or Peru.

One: Nope. Look in John 8. Jesus did it.

Two: *(Eagerly)* Give us another! This is fun.

One: How about "Evangelistic Team Holds Picnic. Five Thousand Attend"?

Two: Was it Billy Graham?

Three: No. Even I get that one. The boy with the loaves and fishes.

One: Right! Try this one: "After Forty Years, Murderer Returns to Scene of Crime."

Three: Is this one *real?*

One: Of course. They are all real.

Three: I mean—well, it sounds like a feature story today.

One: It's in Exodus 4 about Moses coming back to lead the Israelites out of Egypt.

Three: *(Surprised)* He was a *murderer?*

Two: Sure. Remember he killed an Egyptian and ran away for forty years.

One: Try this one: "Local Fisherman Rescued From Sea."

Three: Now that one is *not old!*

One: Are you sure? What about Jesus rescuing Peter when Peter tried to walk on water? Look in Matthew 14 if you don't believe me.

Three: Oh, I believe you. I just don't trust you!

One: Is this a late headline or another from the Bible:

"Farmer's Son Makes Lucky Shot"?

Three: I get it.

Two: I don't.

Three: David when he nailed Goliath

Two: Oh, yeah. Give us another.

One: Only one more because we'll be late for Bible study: "Governor Pardons Criminal."

Three: That could be right now.

One: But it wasn't. Look in Matthew 27 about Pilate pardoning Barabbas.

Three: I still say it could be today.

Two: All those headlines could be today.

One: How about coming with us now?

Three: Well—all right. For a while anyway. Until I see if I like it.

Two: That's being picky! You wanted something relevant and he showed you you could make a whole newpaper out of the Bible!

Three: (*Stubbornly*) Not quite! What about the *comic* section? Huh?

Two: I guess not. You've got us there.

One: Oh, I don't know about that! (*Dramatically*) Picture this—First frame: Jonah overcome with the hot sun. Second frame, a gourd vine growing up over his manger shelter and Jonah relaxing *blissfully*. Third frame, a worm devouring the gourd vine and Jonah shouting *angrily* to heaven, "Why do you let a worm eat *my vine?*" Fourth frame: Jonah *cowering* while a hugh voice thunders, "WHOSE VINE?"

Three: (*Scoffing*) That's not in the Bible!

One: Oh, yes it is! Come on and I'll show you! (*All three puppets leave*)

There Once Were Two Men

by Don Blackley

The Storyteller, Barney, Clarence

Storyteller: There once were two men from Iberia
Who visited a fine cafeteria,
Though starving for lunch, seemed a not-so-wise bunch
When they entered the fine cafeteria. (*Exits. Two businessmen enter*)

Barney: I've heard a lot about this place, Clarence. They have some great food.

Clarence: Yes sir. And I'm starved. Won't my Gloria be mad when she finds I came to such a nice place for lunch?

Barney: Yeah, Mamie too! But, you know, my Mamie can stand to miss a meal or two. Ha! Ha!

Clarence: You'd better not let Mamie hear you say that. Here we are . . . (*Moves as if in a cafeteria line*) Boy, those salads look delicious. Look at this nice big garden salad. What'll it be for you Barney?

Barney: I'm not having salad today.

Clarence: Check these vegetables. Have you ever seen healthier eggplant?

Barney: Well, I never scrutinized an egg . . .

Clarence: And what do you think of the broccoli with the cheese sauce?

Barney: It can't compare to that big hunk of roast beef dead ahead. It smells delicious! You gonna get some of that, Clarence?

Clarence: Think I'll pass on the roast today. But I'm going to get one of these!

Barney: What's that?

Clarence: The Calorie King. It's a block of fudge ice cream, covered with a scoop of marshmallow cream and a half cup of pecans.

Barney: Well that goop and a glass of water isn't a very balanced meal!

Clarence: It's just as balanced as that patty of butter and slice of dill pickle you've got there. Come on. Let's find a table.

Barney: This is some nice cafeteria . . . (*They exit*)

Storyteller: (*Enters*)
There once were two men from our city,
Who joined our fair church, oh, so pretty,
Though needing the Bible, they continued to die,
And missed Sunday School's nitty-gritty! (*Exit Barney and Enter Clarence*)

Barney: Clarence, I'm really proud of our church. Did you know that my great-grandfather helped clear the ground where this building stands?

Clarence: No kidding? I'm a pretty new member here. What is it that keeps this church growing and alive?

Barney: No question about it. (*Proudly*) It's giving top priority to Bible study. (*Gestures*) See that fellow going there?

Clarence: Yeah.

Barney: He teaches our age-group in one of the men's classes. His wife tells me he begins studying on Monday for the next week.

Clarence: You're not serious.

Barney: Yes, I am. We have a whole library just crammed full of study helps and audiovisual equipment. Our teachers use them all the time.

Clarence: What about the kids?

Barney: They get the very best. Why, we had a whole bus load of children and young people's teachers go to a week of training last summer. They really can make Bible study interesting and fun for the kids. *(Bell or buzzer rings)*

Clarence: We really let the time get away from us. Let's get to Sunday School.

Barney: All right. I'll come along and get a cup of coffee. Then why don't you run up to the historical closet with me during class? I promised my wife I'd look up the year her Aunt Jessie started teaching Sunday School here. Yes sir, we sure have a fine Sunday School! *(Both exit as Storyteller enters)*

Storyteller: Now you've heard my unbelieveable tales,
How that Barney and Clarence have failed
To have good sense about beans, and the Sunday School scene,

What a sad, what a miserable tale!

Though possessed with unflagging charm,
Let me twist your spiritual arm,
To give study your best and to grow with the rest,
I can promise it'll do you no harm.

Now just this one final petition,
Because all of us are deficient
In biblical lore, come and study some more,
A word to the wise is sufficient.

Not Reading Your Bible Is Like . . .

by Don Blackley

(Use as many different puppets as possible)

(Narrator is offstage. Puppets pop up one at a time to speak, then vanish again)

Narrator: Having a Bible and not reading it daily is like. . .

Puppet One: Getting fitted for bifocals and taking them off everytime you want to see something.

Narrator: Having a Bible and not reading it daily is like. . .

Puppet Two: Buying a tractor and plow and using it for shade to rest in as you break the ground with a spade.

Narrator: Having a Bible and not reading it daily is like. . .

Puppet Three: Really dumb!

Narrator: Having a Bible and not reading it daily is like. . .

Puppet Four: Owning a new rifle and going bear hunting with a switch.

Narrator: Having a Bible and not reading it daily is like. . .

Puppet One: Having a Ferrari parked in the garage and walking everywhere you go.

Narrator: Having a Bible and not reading it daily is like. . .

Puppet Two: Going to the movie and watching the popcorn machine.

Narrator: Having a Bible and not reading it daily is like. . .

Puppet Three: Really dumb!

Narrator: Having a Bible and not reading it daily is like. . .

Puppet Five: Owning a new twenty-five-inch color television set and never plugging it in to electricity.

Narrator: Having a Bible and not reading it daily is like. . .

Puppet Two: Having a new dishwasher and letting your German shepherd lick your dishes clean.

Narrator: Having a Bible and not reading it daily is like. . .

Puppet One: Standing by the telephone and yelling at your neighbor down the street.

Narrator: Having a Bible and not reading it daily is like. . .

Puppet Four: Sitting down to a table of food and eating the tablecloth.

Narrator: Having a Bible and not reading it daily is like. . .

Puppet One: Owning a motorboat and training your goldfish to pull you on water skis.

Narrator: Having a Bible and not reading it daily is like. . .

Puppet Two: Making a puppet, dressing it up, and then never putting your hand inside it. *(Stays up in position and looks at Number Three)*

Puppet Three: Now you've quit preaching and gone to meddling!

(All puppets jump up into position)

All: Having a Bible and not reading it daily is like . . . really dumb! *(All exit)*

Daily Bible Jogging

by Don Blackley

Clyde Ankle (reporter with microphone), Ronnie Runner

Ronnie Runner (Bible in hand)

Clyde Ankle: Good morning, ladies and gentlemen. This is your on-the-street reporter, Clyde Ankle, reporting for station F-I-N-K. We're looking for an interesting interview here on Mulch Avenue this morning. I hope it turns out a little better than yesterday morning when I was run over by an angry street cleaner. That wasn't so bad though. The brushes on the cleaner gave me a free shoeshine. *(Ronnie Runner comes jogging up)* Here comes an interesting looking gentleman now. *(He runs past audience, moving up and down as if actually running)* Sir, sir would you stop a minute?

Ronnie Runner: Nope, don't have time.

Clyde Ankle: But sir, I'm Clyde Ankle, ace reporter for station F-I-N-K. I'd like to interview you.

Ronnie Runner: If you're going to interview me, you're going to have to keep moving right along.

Clyde Ankle: I can see that you're out getting your daily constitutional. What's your name?

Ronnie Runner: My name is Ronnie Runner. And I'm not just getting my constitutional. I'm doing my daily Bible jogging.

Clyde Ankle: Your daily what?

Ronnie Runner: My daily Bible jogging.

Clyde Ankle: What's that? It sounds like some sort of athletic religious experience.

Ronnie Runner: You might say that. I'm the kind of guy that has to really get disciplined if I'm going to stay consistent in something.

Clyde Ankle: What's that got to do with daily Bible jogging?

Ronnie Runner: Everything! For the longest time I've been a consistent jogger, but I never could really hang in there when it came to reading the Bible. So I decided to apply some of my consistency in running to my Bible study.

Clyde Ankle: So now you read the Bible while you're running?

Ronnie Runner: Right! Haven't missed a morning in two years.

Clyde Ankle: Aren't there some problems about combining the two activities?

Ronnie Runner: Sure. Some minor ones. For example, I probably have the sweatiest book of Psalms in the city.

Clyde Ankle: I see. *(Panting and out of breath now)* But it seems to me that this is highly dangerous for you.

Ronnie Runner: How's that?

Clyde Ankle: *(Panting desperately)* I would think you'd be run over by a semi or trip and fall in a hole.

Ronnie Runner: Nope, never had any trouble. *(Immediately trips and falls with a great deal of movement and noise . . . then slowly drags himself back up over the edge of the stage area)*

Clyde Ankle: *(Stops running and leans down to complete the interview)* Aha! I knew this was a dangerous thing for you to do. Now you've really messed yourself up. I warned you! I knew it would finally catch up with you! *(Pause)* By the way, how did you happen to fall just now?

Ronnie Runner: *(Really steamed about the situation, but talking very patiently and sweetly)* I just happened to trip over *(Then nearly screams)* YOUR STUPID MIC-ROPHONE CABLE! *(He jumps up and chases the reporter off the stage)*

A List of Sins

by Sarah Walton Miller

Two Puppets

One: *(Pleasantly)* Have you studied your Bible lesson today?

Two: *(Crossly)* Naturally! I always study my lesson, don't I?

One: *(Surprised at the temper)* How would I know?

Two: Well, I do!

One: Good. It's about sin.

Two: *(Impatiently)* I know, I know!

One: Anger, malice, wrath, and foul talk.

Two: I *know*, I *said*, didn't I? *Didn't* I?

One: *(Miffed)* Well, you needn't get so huffy.

Two: *(Angrily)* Who's huffy? Who's huffy?

One: *You* are.

Two: *(Yells)* I am not!

One: *(A little angry himself)* What do *you* call it then?

Two: You make me *tired*! Badgering me about—about *trivia*!

One: *(Surprised)* Trivia? The *Bible*?

Two: *(Angry)* There you go again!

One: *(Now angry)* There I go again *what*? Now, look here. . .

Two: *(Yells)* Now look—you shut up!

One: I won't shut up! I have as much right to talk as you do!

Two: *(Yells) Talk*, then! But do it somewhere else! You're a *bore*!

One: *(Shocked)* Oooh! What you said! *Foul language*!

Two: Get out of here! Go pester *Leslie*!

One: Okay, if that's the way you feel. But what about Leslie?

Two: *(Spitefully)* Just ask Leslie what happened after the party at Martin's. Just see what you think of Leslie *then*!

One: Okay, what happened?

Two: How should I know? But Henry said *I* ought to ask, and so I knew right off it *had* to be something *bad*.

One: And that's *all*?

Two: *(Spitefully)* Well, I have *suspicions*. I told Shelly it could be anything—drugs, drink—the works. I never have liked Leslie and certainly don't intend associating with someone who poses as a goody-goody while all the time—well! It isn't for *me* to say!

One: *(Sternly)* Seems to me you've already said it! Suppose Leslie is innocent?

Two: *(Annoyed)* Oh, go—study your lesson!

One: You mean the one about anger, wrath, malice, foul talk, and slander? *(They leave)*

Get Up, Melvin!

by J. B. Collingsworth

Agnes, Melvin

(Alarm clock goes off. Agnes turns it off and yawns)

Agnes: Wake up, Melvin. Hurry and get up. We've got to go to church. Come on, let's go!

Melvin: Oh, go back to sleep, Agnes. We've got plenty of time; besides, who wants to go to Sunday School anyhow?

Agnes: We don't have plenty of time. We have to hurry. Don't you know what today is?

Melvin: *(Sarcastically)* Yes, Agnes today is Sunday—the only day that I have to sleep late. It's also the day after Saturday and the day before Monday. It passes fast enough as it is without having to get up at the crack of dawn. Now would you please let me go back to sleep?

Agnes: No, Melvin, today is not just Sunday. Today is Youth Sunday at the church. We have got to get to church so that the kids can get to the classes they have to teach. They are to be in charge of everything—all the offices will be filled by the young people as well as the choir. We will be hearing one of the young men preach this morning, and tonight they will be doing two dramas and a puppet show. They're excited and have been up and dressed for an hour, so come on. *(Agnes tries to grab Melvin)*

Melvin: Do you mean our kids are going to do all of that?

Agnes: Sure, Melvin, isn't that great? They are really taking an active part for a change. I think that it's wonderful, don't you?

Melvin: Sure, sounds grand, but Agnes, couldn't I sleep just five more minutes? *(Agnes picks up rolling pin and hits Melvin over the head several times)* Okay, I'm up, I'm up, I'm up! *(He exits)*

Agnes: I hope that you won't be as hard to get to Youth Sunday as Melvin. Be here next Sunday—the kids have a real treat in store for you!

Not All Alone*

by Sarah Walton Miller

Four Puppets, Cooperative Program

One: *(Enters, marches back and forth, much agitated)* Woe is me! Woe is me! Oh, Oh! Woe is me! Woe, woe! *(Continues until interrupted)*

Two: *(Enters and watches, interrupts)* Friend! You seem to be in trouble.

One: *(Still moving)* True, true, Woe is me! Oh, oh!

Two: What seems to be the problem?

One: *(wailing)* I am a new Christian!

Two: Congratulations! You should be rejoicing.

One: You don't understand! I read that Jesus wants me to go into all the world and preach the gospel to every creature!

Two: Sounds right to me.

One: It *is* right. But what shall I do?

Two: Go, I guess.

One: Oh, woe is me! I can't! Not all by myself. Do you know how big the world is? Do you know how many years it would take me to cover the entire world?

Two: *(Piously)* You should live so long!

One: That's right Oh, oh, woe is me! *(Continues lamenting. Three enters and watches. Speaks to two)*

Three: What's wrong with him (her)?

Two: He can't go into *all* the world and preach the gospel to every creature.

Three: Oh?

Two: It's too big.

Three: So?

Two: It bugs him.

One: *(Dramatically)* Alas and alack, talking behind my back! That's not all. Not only am I unable to go into all the world but I cannot teach men everywhere to observe all things that God has commanded, either. Not alone I can't.

Three: No indeed.

Two: Impossible.

One: There are billions of people. In the cities, in the country, on mountains and deserts, on ships and in hospitals. . .

Two: Not to mention a few in jails here and there.

One: *(Wailing)* I can't even *find* them all! Much less *teach* them. Alas and alack! Alas and alack!

Three: You forgot "woe is me."

One: Woe is me! And alas and alack! *(Repeats. Four enters and watches. Approaches three)*

Four: What's the matter with him?

Three: He can't teach men everywhere to observe all things God has commanded, for one thing.

Two: For another, he can't go into all the world to preach the gospel to every creature.

Four: And this bugs him?

Two: He's *frustrated*, friend!

Three: He's *miserable*!

One: *(Wailing)* Not only am I unable to go into the whole world and preach the gospel and teach all men everywhere to observe all things God has commanded, but I cannot heal the sick, feed the orphaned, or care for the aged at home and abroad, either! Not alone, I can't. Besides, I don't know how to do these things. And I haven't the money.

Four: True, true.

One: Woe is me! Alas and alack!

OTHERS: Woe is him! Alas and alack! *(Repeat, PUPPET wearing hat labeled "Cooperative Program" enters)*

Cooperative Program: Here! Here! What's all the fuss?

Two: *(Dramatically)* This poor creature can't go into all the world and preach the gospel. Not alone he can't.

Three: Nor teach all men everywhere to observe all things God has commanded. Not alone he can't.

Four: Nor heal the sick, feed the orphaned, and care for the aged at home and abroad. Not alone he can't.

Cooperative Program: Fiddle-faddle! What's he trying to do it all alone for?

One: Because God said. . .

Cooperative Program: *(impatiently)* I know what God said. But he didn't tell us *how* we are to do things. Haven't you ever heard of the Cooperative Program?

One: *(Blankly)* Co-op-er-a-tive Program? What's that?

Cooperátive Program: It's a way for all the churches to pool their money and all work together to help people to go into all the world to preach and teach everywhere, and heal, and feed, and tend! The Cooperative Program!

One: *(marveling, bobbing up and down)* What will they think of next? Goody, goody! Joy, joy! Bliss, bliss! Bliss and joy! *(Exits)*

Two: Well there goes old "Woe is me."

Three: To say nothing of "Alas and alack."

Four: *(sighs sentimentally)* I always did like happy endings!

Cooperative Program: By the way, I've been meaning to talk to you three about your churches *raising* their percentage of giving. . . *(Numbers two, three and four exit quickly)*

Cooperative Program: Wait! I want to talk to you about tithing! *(Exits)*

Missions Everywhere

by John Stell

Teacher, Boy, Girl

Teacher: Boys and girls, I want your close attention. Our lesson today is very special. "Missions around the world."

Boy: Teacher, are we going to take another Lottie Moon offering?

Teacher: No. That will not be done till next Christmas. We give for mission causes through the Cooperative Program all year round—every week.

Girl: I could save some of my allowance and give to a special offering for the missionaries.

Teacher: Let me explain the Cooperative Program to you. Each week as you bring your tithes and offerings to church, it is added to the tithes from all our church members. Part of the money received each Sunday in our church is sent to our state Baptist office where it is added to the money sent from all other Baptist churches in our state. Our state Baptist office sends the largest portion of the money received from all the churches in our state to the Southern Baptist offices for the Cooperative Program where it is added to money sent from state offices all over the United States. So you see, we actually *co-operate* with people all over the

United States to support our missionaries' activities in Oklahoma, the United States and over all the world. When we give our money, it really goes around the world.

Boy: You mean even if I only give a dime?

Teacher: Yes! A part of your dime will make its way into many missions activities. We have over 2,600 missionaries in over seventy foreign countries around the world. There are also many missions projects here in our own state and in all of the other forty-nine states too.

Girl: Wow! That is *terrific*! Just think, Tommy—we support missions not only by special emphasis offerings—but regularly through our church budget.

Boy: Yea, and Mr. Bunch says this has been going on for *fifty years*. How long is fifty years anyway Susie?

Girl: I don't know—I think it's. . .

Teacher: Boys and girls, it is a long time. But most of all, it is far-reaching. I'm glad that a portion of the tithe I bring to God's house goes for such a well planned and worthy missions program.

18

The Missing Link

by Carl Marder

Eddy, Burt, Snoozer, Sissy

(Eddy, Burt, and Snoozer appear playing catch. The ball can be on a string or a stick painted black)

Eddy: Get ready, Burt. Here's my fast ball with a double curve. *(Throws it)*

Burt: *(Catching it and throwing it)* And here's my slow ball with a surprise upward turn.

Snoozer: *(Catching it and throwing it)* And now comes my high ball with its sneak return. *(The ball goes high and lodges in a tree branch overhead)*

Eddy and Burt: Awww, Snooze. You threw it into the tree.

Burt: Your dumb "high ball" that never returned.

Eddy: It's almost time to leave for Sunday School and we have to waste time getting the ball down.

Burt: Instead of practicing. And the game's tomorrow.

Snoozer: Stop griping. How are we going to get it down? We can't shimmy up the tree in our Sunday clothes.

Burt: Get some rocks and throw them. Maybe we can knock it loose. *(Pantomime throwing rocks)*

Eddy: I can't get near it.

Snoozer: It's wedged in the tree too tight.

Burt: You got it up there. You think of a way to get it down.

Snoozer: What about a stick or a pole to knock it out.

Eddy: We don't have a stick that long.

Burt: I'll go get a ladder.

Eddy: Your ladder is only five feet tall and the ball is three times that high.

Burt: We could make a ladder out of ourselves.

Snoozer: What!

Burt: Like in the circus. We could stand on each other's shoulders. The three of us would be tall enough to reach it.

Eddy: Dubs on being on top.

Snoozer: We have to put the smallest on top and the biggest on bottom.

Burt: I know. Don't tell me. That means I'm on bottom.

Snoozer: And I'm on top.

Eddy: I always end up in the middle.

Burt: We're wasting time we could be practicing. Let's go do it. *(Puppeteers in black sleeves maneuver Eddy up on Burt, then Snoozer to the top.)*

Ad-lib: Hey, that's my ear you're on . . . Watch out and don't tear my shirt . . . Keep your toes out of my nose.

Snoozer: I'm up. Everyone hold still, I think I can reach it. I'll hang on to this branch and shake it loose.

(Offstage)

Sissy: Eddy, it's time for Sunday School. Dad says come now.

Eddy: I can't. I'm helping Snoozer.

Burt: You're not helping unless you stop wiggling.

Sissy: *(Enters)* You better come or you're going to get in trouble. Dad says we have to leave now. It's late.

Eddy: How you comin', Snooze?

Snoozer: It's stuck.

Eddy: Well, hurry.

Snoozer: I can't.

Burt: Be still.

Sissy: We're leaving.

Eddy: Tell Dad I just can't come now. They need me. If I weren't here there'd be a big gap between Snooze and Burt.

Sissy: I'll tell him, but hurry! *(Exits)*

Snoozer: Here it comes . . . it's loose. *(Ball drops to the ground)*

All: Hurrah! *(They climb down)*

Burt: It's a good thing it came loose. I was about to collapse with both of you on top of me.

Eddy: But if the ball had stayed up there and I had left for Sunday School, you'd have been in trouble.

Snooze: Let's practice some more.

Eddy: I've gotta go to Sunday School.

Burt: All you need to do is send your envelope. My Dad says all the church wants is your money.

Eddy: My Dad says . . . they need me. Just like you and Snooze did. A ladder or a stick or a rock wouldn't do. You needed me. Well, so does God. See you tomorrow at the game. *(Exits)*

STEWARDSHIP PLUS

by John Stell

Two Puppets

(First puppet enters humming. Knock at door)
One: Come in please.
Two: Hi, you must be Mr. Jones? I am Frank Earnest from the office of Internal Revenue Audits.
One: Well I am glad to meet you Mr. Earnest. Won't you have a seat?
Two: Let me get right to the point Mr. Jones. I have been checking your return for this past year, and I have one area that I want to check with you on.
One: Fine, Sir, any way that I can help you, I will.
Two: You list as your gross income for last year just under five thousand dollars, and you have listed under contributions an amount of six hundred and thirty-five dollars. Now this is in the limit all right, but I just want to know if you can prove this amount for our records?
One: Of course, Let me see, I have those receipts right here in my file folder . . . here it is Believer's Baptist Church list of contributions for 1974. . . .
Two: Uh huh, hmmm . . . yes, that is sufficient all right. I am sure that you are being honest with the government. Thank you very much Mr. Jones.
One: You're welcome. Mr. Earnest I'd like to invite you to attend our church sometime.
Two: Thanks but I belong to a church myself.
One: Oh!—Excuse me. That thought never occurred to me.

A Nonroutine Announcement

by Sarah Walton Miller

Prunella, Wilbur

Prunella: *(Loudly)* Wilbur! Come out! *(Wilbur enters)*
Wilbur: *(Listlessly)* Oh, it's you. *(In a mocking way)* You want me to come to the church. Why?
Prunella: *(Excited)* Because you'll like what's going to happen!
Wilbur: *(Unimpressed)* What, for instance?
Prunella: *(Eagerly)* The choir is giving a b-i-g concert with orchestra and lots of things!
Wilbur: *(Sneering)* La, la, la! Anything else?
Prunella: *(Not so enthusiastic now)* Welll . . . there's going to be a *party*, a scrumptious party!
Wilbur: Ho-hum. Is that all?
Prunella: *(Definitely squelched by now)* Uh—no. We're planning a trip through the Ozarks.
Wilbur: *(Nastily)* Well, have fun! Is that all?
Prunella: *(In despair)* All that would interest you. Nothing else is going on except _____ . *(Insert name of activity. Wilbur goes into an excited frenzy, jumping up and down, and screaming excitedly)*
Wilbur: _____ ? Oh, why didn't you say so in the first place! _____ ! O glorious day! Come on Prunella! Hurry! Hurry! *(He leaves fast. Prunella looks after him a moment, then to the audience)*
Prunella: I sometimes think that boy's not bright! *(She leaves)*

20

Food Fantasteec!

by Don Blackley

Announcer, Chef Bahlonee

(The Announcer is in typical television announcer attire)
(Chef Bahlonee is a French cook, in white shirt, chef's hat, and dark moustache. Spoon attached to movable hand)
(Big bowl center stage. Taped or live music tapers out as dialogue begins.)

Announcer: Good evening ladies and gentlemen. Welcome to another fun-filled half-hour of "Food Fantasteec," the first religious food program on television. You ask me why it's religious food? Because it's one of the few cook shows that can turn a gorgeous sirloin steak into a burnt offering. Now welcome, if you will, our host: not the regular run-of-the-mill "galloping gourmet," but our own "creeping cookie," Chef Bahlonee! *(Applause)*

Chef Bahlonee: *(Enters waving spoon)* Thank you, thank you! We're glad you tuned in again. I'm sure you'll notice that since last week we've been able to successfully remove all zee spaghetti sauce from zee walls and ceiling. *(Gestures grandly)* Now on with zee show. Tonight we're going to create a culinary masterpiece. It's called zee "Happy Growing Church Cobbler." It is not an easy dish to create because of zee need for so many different ingredients. And they must also be blended in just zee right amounts. *(Looking at announcer)* Are we ready to proceed?

Announcer: That we are. We've tried to put together all the necessary condiments for this wonderful dish.

Chef Bahlonee: Fine. Zee very first ingredient for "Happy Growing Church Cobbler" is a large, healthy cluster of people. Big ones, little ones, smart ones, slow ones, rich ones, poor ones. This will give the cobbler a wider range of flavor. It will not hurt zee cobbler if your people are of a different shade or tint either. Zee people are your basic ingredient. But just as important, stir in a bushel of love. *(Announcer helps, as chief dips many times to put "love" in the bowl)*

Announcer: Now Chef Bahlonee, this love looks a little deeper in color than your "everyday, buy-it-at-the-corner-market love."

Chef Bahlonee: I'm glad you mentioned that. This is a special kind of love. It is called "unselfeesh" or sacrificial love. It has zee peculiar ability to blend all of these people together into a nice smooth texture. Look! Isn't that pretty? *(Announcer looks and nods his head)*

Announcer: What's next?

Chef Bahlonee: Pass me zee Bible study and training. You need to work quite a bit of this Bible study into zee mixture. *(Stirs mixture)* It gives zee whole dish consistency. In fact, you can add as much as you like and not ruin zee dish. But without it . . . Yuck! Zee cobbler is too flat! Now, add a pinch of finely ground sense of humor. Put in three cups of prayer and meditation. *(Stirring wildly now)* Add a pound of personal ministry! Magnifique! *(Throws spoon up in air)* We are close to a successful dish! Stir in two cups of fellowship and caring, and then we have one last ingredient. Hand me zee visitation.

Announcer: The what?

Chef Bahlonee: Zee visitation!

Announcer: What's it look like? *(Looking around)*

Chef Bahlonee: *(Irritated)* What does it look like? It comes in a big container marked "Handle with Care —Contents Valuable." Where is it?

Announcer: I don't know. *(Looking at audience nervously)* Folks, just a little delay here while we find the visitation. *(To the chef)* I really haven't seen any around here in a long time.

Chef Bahlonee: What? We can't make zee "Happy Growing Church Cobbler" without it! Surely there's a little bit left around here. It's also called "outreach" by some of the younger chefs. It comes in a different box but it is all zee same stuff.

Announcer: Well, I've combed this kitchen high and low and there isn't any visitation or outreach here.

Chef Bahlonee: *(Beginning to sob)* My masterpiece, my fantastic creation all ruined! *(Crying now)* It will never be right without zee visitation.

Announcer: Can't we substitute something for it? *(Looking around)* How about some of this stuff called stewardship?

Chef Bahlonee: No, no, no! Don't you understand! There is no substitute!

Announcer: Well I see by the old clock on the wall we're about out of time. . . .

Chef Bahlonee: If any of you in zee viewing audience know where we can get some more visitation or outreach, please call the sponsor of our program and volunteer this information. Perhaps you have a little in your own supplies. This recipe can wait a little while before adding it, but if we go very long the whole batch of "Happy Growing Church Cobbler" will spoil.

Announcer: *(Theme music begins)* Thanks for tuning in again on another edition of "Food Fantasteec," featuring Chef Bahlonee and his epicurean delights!

Chef Bahlonee: Just to think, ruined because we didn't have enough visitation. What are we going to do?

Announcer: *(Trying to console, helping him offstage)* Would it help to stir in a little summer mission trip? *(Exit)*

Visions

by Joan King

Harvey, Charlie, Bernard

Harvey: Charlie, have you noticed how funny Bernard has been acting?

Charlie: Yeah, look at him now. He's wearing earmuffs and dark glasses! He looks like he doesn't know if it's summer or winter!

Bernard: Hey, get quiet over there! Can't you see that I'm trying to have a vision?

Harvey: You're trying to what?

Bernard: I'm trying to have a vision: So QUIET!

Harvey: Charlie, what's a vision? Is it a terrible disease of the eyes and ears?

Charlie: I don't know, Harvey. I just know I don't want to catch one if I have to wear earmuffs and dark glasses.

Harvey: Bernard, tell us what a vision is.

Bernard: It's what Paul saw on his way to Damascus. After his vision, he became a great Christian witness. That's what I want to be.

Harvey: Was Paul wearing earmuffs and dark glasses when he saw a vision? I thought it was too hot where Paul lived to wear earmuffs.

Charlie: Yeah. And why are you wearing dark glasses? Surely Paul didn't wear dark glasses. Nobody owned dark glasses way back then.

Bernard: Well, Paul was blinded when he saw his vision. I thought the sunglasses might get me in the mood. Doesn't that make sense?

Harvey: No more than anything else you've said. And why are you wearing those earmuffs?

Bernard: So I can concentrate. Some people around here are so noisy that a person can't even think. Excuse me now. I've got to get back to concentrating on my vision.

Harvey: Charlie, I don't know very much about visions, but don't you think Bernard could become a Christian witness without wearing all that getup?

Charlie: Yeah, I think maybe Bernard is doing like a lot of Christians—trying to be a witness without the Lord's help.

Harvey: Hey, Bernard.

Bernard: Oh, no. You again. I'm never going to accomplish anything.

Harvey: That's right, Bernard. You'll never accomplish anything in Christian witnessing—by yourself.

Charlie: Harvey's right. We have to listen to the Lord the way Paul did and then continually pray that the Lord will call us to do his will.

Harvey: Bernard, why don't you forget about earmuffs, sunglasses, and visions. Ask the Lord to lead you as a witness.

Charlie: That's right, Bernard. You're too involved in the . . . mechanics of being a witness.

Bernard: Maybe you're right. I've been so involved in getting a message from God the way Paul did, that I didn't take time to stop and listen to God's spirit speak to me. You two have helped me. You've been witnessing to me about witnessing.

Charlie: And we know a song to help you remember what we've talked about. *(Sing any song on witnessing)*

Visitation Excuses

by Don Blackley

Puppet Singer(s) (one or more puppets to sing the theme), Pastor and Lawyer (one puppet plays both parts), Mr. I. M. Able, Miss Faithful, Buddy and Judge (one puppet plays both parts, use black robe for judge's costume)

(Piano introduction begins—"For He's a Jolly Good Fellow" as Singers enter)

Singers: *(to the tune of "For He's a Jolly Good Fellow")*
We get a lot of excuses,
We get a lot of excuses,
Dear Pastor, you'll have to excuse me,
I don't have the time to go.
(Singers repeat last phrase as they exit)
I don't have the time to go.
I don't have the time to go.

(Pastor enters and stands greeting folks leaving church service. Miss Faithful enters)

Pastor: It's good to see you in church this morning Miss Faithful. You're looking well.

Miss Faithful: Well Pastor, I'm going to go home and shine my shoes. You stepped all over my toes this morning in that message on witnessing. But I did enjoy it.

Pastor: Thank you Miss Faithful. I needed to hear that sermon myself. *(Mr. Able enters)* Good-bye now. *(Miss Faithful exits)* Brother Able I'm glad you came out this exit. I needed to ask you something.

I. M. Able: Sure pastor. What is it?

Pastor: Will you go visiting with me this *(visitation night)*? I need a partner to go along with me.

I. M. Able: Oh . . . uh . . . let's see. I'd sure like to, but I think I have something real important going that night. Is it P.T.A. committee meeting? Or is that the night my wife's invited her old school chum over? Sorry Pastor, I can't quite recall, but I'm sure I'm busy. Maybe some other time.

Pastor: Sure Brother Able. Perhaps you can go along some other time. *(Pastor exits. I. M. Able starts to exit. Buddy enters)*

Buddy: Hold up I. M. I want to talk to you.

I. M. Able: Sure Buddy. What's new?

Buddy: Last week my boss gave me two tickets to _____ . *(Fill in any event at this time of year—concert, football game . . .)* Why don't you go with me _____ ? *(visitation night)*

I. M. Able: Boy, oh boy, would I like to do that! Sure, I don't know of a thing that could stop me. Wild horses could not keep me away! *(They exit chatting excitedly. Singers enter)*

Singers: We get a lot of excuses,
We get a lot of excuses,
Dear Pastor, you'll have to excuse me,
I wouldn't know what to say!
(Singers repeat last phrase as they exit)
I wouldn't know what to say.
I wouldn't know what to say.

(Court scene. Judge puppet behind high wooden desk)

Judge: Now, Mr. Able, tell us what you saw that day.

I. M. Able: Well Judge, I've got to tell you I'm rather nervous about being here.

Judge: That's understandable, since this *is* your first time to testify in a court.

I. M. Able: I don't know anything about law. I don't even get to watch the old Perry Mason reruns on television.

Judge: That's perfectly all right Mr. Able. All we want you to do is recount what you saw on that day.

I. M. Able: But I don't know all the technicalities of the law, Judge. I don't know a *habeas corpus* from a court clerk.

Judge: Mr. Able . . .

I. M. Able: The closest I've ever been to the law is when the Sheriff backed into my car downtown one day.

Judge: Mr. Able. Your ability to testify in a court of law does not hinge upon your complete understanding of the intricacies of the judicial process. It is very simple. You must simply tell the court what you saw from your vantage point. You do not have to defend it. You do not have to explain it. You simply have to state what you saw take place. Now that you understand that . . . let's break for lunch! *(All exit)*

(Singers enter)

Singers: We all have our excuses,
We all have our excuses,
But Pastor, you can count on me.
I'm willing to visit now!
I'm willing to visit now!
(Singers build to a climactic ending)
I'm willing to visit now! *(Exit)*

23

Let's Promote that Church Library

by Sarah Walton Miller

Book Puppets, Lending Card Puppets, Two Regular Puppets

(The two puppets appear at one side, look around and at each other, silently. We hear voices, muttering at first. Then we understand words as the books begin marching across the stage behind the puppets, and off. We hear such remarks as:)

Thank heaven, I'm back!

Oh joy! I thought I'd *never* be found behind that sofa.

Happy day! That kid was *murder* on me!

You'd never believe what happened to me!

I was in a hospital.

An old man read me twice.

Back to the old shelves, gang!

(Ad-lib other lines until all have marched across. As soon as they have passed, run the "cards," with such remarks as:)

Mine's back! I saw him!

It's been a whole *year*.

Hurry! I can harly wait.

(The two puppets watch this parade, looking at each other now and then and reacting to what they hear. After the last card has gone by, the books come back, going in the opposite direction with such remarks as:)

Well, here we go again!

Isn't it great?

I hope they enjoy me.

I feel sorry for the books that have to stay on the shelf.—*(And other such remarks until all have passed again. Create your own remarks)*

Puppet One: *(Stops the last Book)* Hey! Wait a minute!

Book: Who—me?

One: Didn't I see you just go back into that library?

Book: *(Happily)* That I did!

Two: We saw you!

One: Didn't I hear you say you were *glad* to be back?

Book: That you did!

Two: We heard you!

One: Then why are you so glad to go already?

Book: *(Happily)* That's what library books are *for!* To go out to people.

One: Then why were you so glad to get back?

Two: Yes. Why?

Book: We couldn't very well go *out* until we got *in*, could we?

One: Oh?

Book: You see, sometimes people take us out and then forget to bring us back. That's a *black day!* Woe is me! Alas! Alas!

(Book disappears. The puppets look at each other and then at the audience. There is a pause)

Two: You don't suppose . . . no, no! *These* people wouldn't do that.

One: Well, not on purpose. Remember how happy those books were to be found and returned?

Two: *(Appealing to audience)* Oh, please! Please everybody! Please look around and find those forgotten library books! Make a *book* happy today! Bring it back!

(Books rush back in a group, saying such things as:)

Take *me* out instead!

We want to go home with you for a while!

Reading is fun!

Hurry! Hurry!

(Books rush out. The two puppets look long at each other, then nod and go off in the direction the books went)

That Outreach*

by Sarah Walton Miller

Wilbur, Prunella

(Small, stuffed animal sits near stage in reach of Wilbur. Wilbur enters, sees animal)

Wilbur: Hi! *(No response, he waits, tries again, louder)* Hi! *(Prunella appears)*

Prunella: Wilbur! How marvelous to see you! It's been a long time.

Wilbur: Sure has. What are you doing at the airport?

Prunella: Catching a plane for Glorieta. There's a recreation conference.

Wilbur: I know—that's where I'm headed.

Prunella: What a coincidence!

Wilbur: Isn't it? What's new with you?

Prunella: Oh, I'm busy with an outreach program for my church.

Wilbur: Outreach? What do you mean?

Prunella: We're trying to take the church outside the walls into the community . . . to reach all people on their level. We've got to communicate and let people know we care.

Wilbur: That's great!

Prunella: Isn't it? We'll use various means as we get our people ready to serve?

Wilbur: Such as what means?

Prunella: *(Rattling them off)* Oh—recreation for neighborhood children, classes in English, activities for senior citizens, a class and also recreation for the retarded, day-care nursery, well, whatever will show people we do care and can talk to each other.

Wilbur: That character over there could stand some of your outreach.

Prunella: What character?

Wilbur: That one—in the mod suit.

Prunella: You mean that one just sitting there? He's not doing anything.

Wilbur: I know. That's just it. I smiled at him a while ago and said "Hi" and he just sat there.

Prunella: Not friendly, huh?

Wilbur: Definitely not friendly.

Prunella: Let me try. *(She moves nearer figure, clears throat loudly)* Ah-hem! It's a nice day, isn't it? . . . Isn't it?

Wilbur: *(Loud whisper)* See? I told you so!

Prunella: My friend and I just want to be friendly . . . *(Loses temper)* Well! You could answer me! . . . Get that silly smirk off your face!

Wilbur: *(Moves closer)* Here, now! Are you trying to insult this lady? Or do you think you are too good to speak to us?

Prunella: Of all the stubborn, uncouth, disagreeable—

Wilbur: *(Pushes character over)* Then get out of here if you can't be friendly! Come on, Prunella! *(They pull back, then Prunella speaks)*

Prunella: Look, Wilbur!

Wilbur: What?

Prunella: He's still down. He hasn't moved.

Wilbur: He's just playing for sympathy.

Prunella: Maybe you hurt him?

Wilbur: He didn't holler, he can't be hurt much.

Prunella: Maybe you hurt his feelings—on the inside.

Wilbur: *(Heartily)* Nonsense! No red-blooded American male can be such a sissy!

Prunella: Maybe—maybe he's not American. Maybe he didn't know what you said?

Wilbur: Then why does he go around in our country looking like *us?*

Prunella: Let's go back!

Wilbur: *(Firmly)* Prunella! You are wasting time trying to sympathize with people like that! Come on! Let's go! You can tell me more about your outreach program! *(They exit)*

---

*Indoor/Outdoor Recreation Pack. Nashville: Broadman Press, 1976.

Section II

BIBLE STUDY AND WORSHIP

The Greatest Show on Earth

by Joan King

People in front of stage: Agent, Two Clowns

Puppets: *Alfred,* an inchworm; *Rosemary,* a dog; *Red,* a hound dog; *Mertle; Clown; Henry,* lion tamer; *Lionel,* a lion

Props: Basketball, basketball goal, cage, mirror, mike and stand, big top, sparklers attached to coat hangers.

Alfred: *(Fanfare)* Ladies and Gentlemen, welcome to the "Greatest Show on Earth!" If you would direct your attention to the center ring, our first act—Red and Rosemary, World-Famous Juggling Canines! *(Exit, basketball goal up, basketball is styrofoam ball on end of coat hanger, Music and juggling begins, Agent enters, Rosemary exists after act)*

Agent: This show must be stopped.

Red: What'd we do?

Agent: It's what you didn't do. Where's the ringmaster?

Red: Alfred, Hey Alfred! *(Alfred enters)*

Alfred: Did you call me, Red?

Red: No, I called you Alfred. Yuk, Yuk! Alfred—I think we've got a problem. Actually, you've got a problem and I've got a problem. My problem is that Rosemary's in love with me. She thinks I'm cute.

Alfred: Now listen, Red, if Rosemary is in love with you, she's the one with the problem. Anyway, it sounds like a case of puppy love to me. But, you said I had a problem. What'd ya mean?

Red: That lady said she was going to stop the act.

Alfred: Stop my circus? Stop my circus! Nobody can shut down my circus. It's the greatest show ever produced. Who do you think you are anyway?

Agent: I'm from FIBIC, the Federal Investigation Bureau for International Circuses.

Alfred: Uh. Oh. As I was saying, the only person who could possibly shut down my circus is one of those nice agents from FIBIC. May I help you, Ma'am?

Agent: Yes, I've been observing your performers, and I have discovered that even though they have outstanding talent, they're missing one thing. The title of your circus, "God's Creation Circus" is misleading because love is missing from your acts, and puppy love doesn't count. If you can't find love, I must close the circus. *(Exit)*

Alfred: Rip-off! Rip-off! Somebody's ripped off our love! *(Red and Clown enter)*

Red: What'd she say, Alfred?

Alfred: She said that love is missing from our acts, and I want to know who took it!

Clown: Calm down, Alfred, We'll find it.

Alfred: Calm down? What makes you think I'm upset? I'm completely calm! I'm not upset! *(Runs off and screams)*

Clown: Alfred, why don't you appoint some detectives to start an anywhere—everywhere search?

Alfred: Hey! That's a good idea. Give me a mike. *(Mike stand appears; use reverb on mike)* Attention! Attention everybody! May I have your complete, total, and undivided attention? This is an emergency. I repeat, this is an emergency! Someone has ripped off our love. I repeat, this is a rip-off! I'm appointing all clowns as special agents to conduct an anywhere-everywhere search. Carry on, clowns. *(All exit, lights change, Henry cage, and Lionel enter. Two clowns enter in front of stage)*

Clown: Henry, Henry!

Henry: *(Enters)* you called me?

Clown? Yes. Henry, as special agents, we are on the search for the missing love. Have you seen it?

Henry: Can't say that I have. In fact, I've been too busy training Lionel for his big act to be concerned over such trivial matters. I suggest you check at the monkey act. Lionel and I must get to work. *(Clowns exit; Red enters)*

Red: Henry.

Henry: Yes, Red, another problem?

Red: The same one, Henry. Rosemary's still in love with me.

Henry: Is it she whom the clowns are looking for?

Red: Oh, no. That's not the kind of love they're after. *(Looks around)* Don't tell anybody, Henry, but this is boy-girl love. Yuk.

Henry: Well, my good lad, you're a very talented boy. I'm sure you could form an act of your own and star.

Red: Shucks, Henry, I can't solo yet.

Henry: Confidence, my lad. You must have confidence in your own abilities . . . Your own talent. Observe that fearless beast in the cage. His body possesses power and strength. He's a savage. But fearless as I am, and confident in my abilities to train such a powerhouse, I have developed the greatest lion act in the world.

Red: But, I don't have any confidence. Henry, do you mean, confidence to use my talents, is what I need?

Henry: Yes, confidence like mine that soothed that beast.

Red: Do you think I need confidence with Rosemary?

Henry: What do you mean?

Red: Well, I sort of like her. Now, I didn't say love . . . just like. Is confidence what I need so I can tell her I like her?

Henry: Now, old chap, you've finally hit upon the real problem. You need confidence in yourself; and I, of course, have the solution. Many young ladies admire Henry the lion tamer, so you've come to the expert. What you need, my boy, is a mirror.

Red: A mirror?

Henry: Yes. Stand in front of a mirror and tell yourself all of your good qualities. In a few days you will be confident enough to tell little Rosemary you love her.

Red: I don't love her, Henry, I just like her a lot.

Henry: Yes, yes. Go on now and find your mirror. Lionel and I must get to work. *(Henry exits; mirror appears)*

Red: You have confidence, and charm, and personality . . . and good looks *(Pause)* Well, we'll just skip that one. *(Alfred and clown enter)* And you have intelligence and wit . . .

Alfred: And a cracked skull.

Red: No, Alfred. I'm building up confidence to tell Rosemary I like her.

Clown: Talking to yourself is supposed to help you build courage to tell Rosemary you love her?

Red: I didn't say love, I said like.

Alfred: And I say get to work! Here I'm in the middle of the greatest crisis of my life. An FIBIC agent is about to close down my circus, and what else do I have to cope with? A stupid hound dog who talks to himself in the mirror. I'm going crazy! *(Exits. Mertle enters)*

Red: I think Alfred needs some help. Do you think mirror therapy would help him?

Mertle: I'm not sure, but we need to find a solution to your problem, Red.

Red: I think it's hopeless Mertle.

Mertle: Now, Red. You must try. Has the mirror helped?

Red: It does until I get to the part about good-looking . . . then I feel like I bombed out!

Mertle: Well, Red, at least you're honest. If you're honest in your weaknesses, why not be honest in your strengths?

Red: Oh, I'm not very strong Mertle.

Mertle: Not that kind of strength, Red. People are strong in many different ways. You are afraid of showing your love for Rosemary, as so many people are afraid of showing their love for God. If you really love Rosemary, admit it to yourself, and then you will be able to tell everyone.

Red: Shucks, I'd be embarrassed.

Mertle: That's what's wrong with this circus. A lot of people have love in their hearts, but for some reason, they're not expressing it.

Red: Maybe you're right. I'll try to tell Rosemary.

Mertle: And I'll see if we can't find the love missing from the circus in our hearts. *(They exit) (Mertle enters singing "Love Will Keep Us Together." Then clown enters looking for love)*

Clown: Hey, haven't you heard about the anywhere-everywhere search we're conducting? Somebody has ripped off the love in our circus.

Mertle: That's silly. The love isn't missing.

Clown: The FIBIC inspector says that it is.

Mertle: Well, I suppose if I were in her position, I'd think the same thing. Some of us have really been putting too much emphasis on talent lately.

Clown: If somebody hasn't taken our love, where is it?

Mertle: In your heart. We're all Christians, right?

Clown: Right.

Mertle: When we place our trust in the Lord, he gave us something greater than all of our talents—he gave us love. First Corinthians 13 says: "Though I speak with the tongues of men and of angels, and have not love, I am become as sounding brass, or a tinkling cymbal. And though I have the gift of prophecy, and understand all mysteries, and all knowledge; and though I have all faith, so that I could remove mountains, and have not love, I am nothing. Love bears all things, believes all things, hopes all things, and endures all things. Love never fails."

Clown: So our love isn't missing! We've just been putting a talented performance before a loving performance.

Mertle: That's right. You see, you can have both. If we let the Lord guide us and ask him to bless our talents in a spirit of love we will discover greater joy than we've ever known.

Clown: This is great. Wait till Alfred hears. He's been having nervous breakdowns all afternoon. *(Alfred enters)* Alfred! We've found the problem. Our love has been here all the time.

Alfred: Where? Not in front of me it hasn't. I've looked everywhere. Even frisked everybody who came through the gates.

Clown: But we didn't take time to look within ourselves, Alfred. Our love has been in our hearts all along, covered with pride rather than humility.

Alfred: You know, maybe you're right. But will the FIBIC agent see it? Here she comes now. *(Agent enters)*

Agent: Well, have you found the missing love?

Clown: Yes, ma'am. We found it in our hearts.

Agent: Very good. Now, can you show it in your performance?

Clown: Yes, ma'am. Introduction please, Alfred.

Alfred: Ladies and gentlemen, "The Greatest Show on Earth" presents the grand finale and wishes you good night. *(Puppets all sing "The Melody in My Heart Is Love" from The Old Songs tape. Sparklers in background on last verse)*

A Boy Shares His Lunch

by Don Blackley

Ralph, Billy, Sammy, Sally, Carl

(Lamb puppets sing to "Baa, Baa Black Sheep" nursery rhyme)

Ralph: Hi there, I know you think you were brought here to practice this little routine for the Carol Burnett show, but in reality this was all a little trick played by your friends in order for me to say I'm Ralph Shmedwards, and Billy Baa *(Grandiose)—THIS IS YOUR LIFE!*

Billy: Me? Oh, you're fooling. Not me! Why this is the biggest surprise of my life.

Ralph: Come right over here Billy. We want you to listen to his voice from your past.

Sammy: Billy, from the moment I saw your little black wool frolicking around the pasture, I knew you were going to be something special.

Ralph: Do you recognize that voice?

Billy: Why that's my master! My owner!

Ralph: Here from San Mateo, California, your master and owner, Sammy Shepherd. *(Sammy bounces in and hugs Billy)*

Sammy: Billy, not only were you fun to be around because of your playful ways, but you always faithfully did your part in the flock. Regularly you gave back to me a big bag of that thick black wool.

Billy: Aw, but it wasn't anything. You provided me with food and shelter. And you always came to find me if I wandered off too far from the rest of the flock.

Ralph: Yessir, it's so good to have your master here, Mr. Shepherd. Let's give him a big hand. *(Applause as he exits)* Now Billy, see if this voice brings back memories.

Sally: Remember that time when you were up on that high rocky ledge and stumbled and fell in the cactus?

Billy: I surely do. And I remember that voice. That's my master's wife, Sally Shepherd. *(She runs in—they embrace)*

Sally: Can you recall that evening when you came in from the pasture? We sat and picked cactus needles out of you for several hours?

Billy: I can recall that. You were so kind to me. Whenever I needed a friend you were always there.

Ralph: And remembering that friendship Billy, you always were faithful to share a bag of your wool with Mrs. Shepherd, every time you were shorn. Thank you Mrs. Sally Shepherd for coming to make this evening special. *(Applause as she exits)* Billy you'll have to listen carefully to identify this voice from your past.

Carl: *(Offstage)* Billy, your generosity had quite an impact on my whole family.

Billy: I can't remember. The voice sounds familiar . . . but who . . . ?

Ralph: From your hometown we've flown a neighbor that you don't know very well, but who remembers you vividly, Carl Perkins.

Carl: Hi Billy. Back in our hometown, my family and I lived several miles from the Shepherd ranch. We were really having a hard time making enough money to have food on the table. Billy didn't even know me or my family, but when he heard about our trouble he insisted that he share what he had with us. The most valuable thing he had was his black wool. He shared this with us time after time, enabling us to sell it and buy food for our family. I was just a poor little boy that lived down the road, but Billy cared enough to share so that we could be happy. Thank you, Billy.

Ralph: And thank you Carl Perkins, now a grown-up businessman, but once the poor little boy that lived down the road. Let's give him a hand. *(Applause as he exits)* Well, Billy, it has been exciting tonight to relive your life and see how you shared what you had. What motivated you to want to share with Sammy Shepherd?

Billy: I just had to share with him. He owned me. He's my master.

Ralph: Why did you bother to share with Sally Shepherd?

Billy: Oh, I shared with her because she's my friend. She was always so kind to me. I wanted to say thank you somehow.

Ralph: Yes, but why did you bother to share with Carl Perkins, the little boy down the road? You didn't even know him.

Billy: That's true. I didn't. But I did know that he had great needs in his life and I felt that I just wanted to do my little part in meeting those needs. I believe it was Jesus, the Great Shepherd who said, "If you've done it unto the smallest of these needy persons, you've done it unto me." I like that!

Ralph: And we like you. Billy Baa, THIS IS YOUR LIFE!

Announcer: *(All the characters enter to hug and talk while announcer says . . .)* This Is Your Life has been a Charles Woodson-Bill Rogers production. This is EBS, the Easter Bible School Network. The preceding was pre-recorded, recorded, recorded, recorded. . . . *(Sounds fade as word is repeated)*

Love Your Neighbor*

by Lyn Yarborough

Turtle, Rabbit

Turtle: *(Enters looking toward the sky)* The sun is too bright. I need some sleep. *(Yawn)* If the sun shines in my eyes early in the morning, I can't sleep. *(Spies bricks)* I'll just build a wall out of those bricks and that will keep the sun out of my eyes until later in the day. *(He stacks three bricks, one on top of the other and goes back down)* Now maybe I can get some sleep.

Rabbit: *(Enters, looks around nervously, and sees wall)* Now who built that wall? Now the sun won't shine on my lettuce all afternoon. They won't grow big and tender and juicy and I won't be able to feed my family. *(Unstacks bricks, exits)*

Turtle: *(Enters)* Hey, the sun is in my eyes again. I can't sleep that way. I'll build the wall back. *(He does so)* Now maybe I can get some sleep *(Exits)*

Rabbit: *(Enters)* That wall again. The shade will ruin my lettuce. *(Tears wall down, exits)*

Turtle: *(Enters)* I can't believe it. Here we go again. *(Builds wall, exits)*

Rabbit: *(Enters)* That makes me so mad *(Tears down, exits)*

Turtle: *(Enters)* Something's fishy here! I'm going to hide and see what happens this time. *(Builds wall, goes to one side and waits)*

Rabbit: *(Enters)* This is making me tired. I wish I knew who kept building this wall. *(Starts to tear down wall. Turtle rushes over)*

Turtle: Wait a minute! Who do you think you are, tearing down my wall!

Rabbit: Who do you think you are, putting up a wall so my lettuce won't get any afternoon sun?

Turtle: Well, the sun gets in my eyes early in the morning and I can't sleep. I stay up all night finding bugs and things to eat, and I need sleep early in the morning.

Rabbit: Well, I have to grow this garden so I can feed all my little baby bunny rabbits. What am I going to do when all those little bunnies sit down to the table and there is no lettuce to eat?

Turtle: I don't know, but I am going to build this wall. *(Starts to build)*

Rabbit: No you're not. *(Interferes with turtle. They scuffle back and forth, one saying "No you're not!" The other saying "Oh, yes I am" until finally they stop in exhaustion)*

Turtle: Wait a minute. We're neighbors, aren't we? There's no reason for us to fight. We've always been good friends, haven't we?

Rabbit: Up until now, anyway.

Turtle: Well, let's see what we can do. Maybe if we put the bricks side by side, they would be tall enough to keep the sun out of my eyes early in the morning, and low enough for the afternoon sun to shine on your lettuce.

Rabbit: That's an idea. Here, let me help. *(They work together to put bricks side by side, words are on bricks: Love Your Neighbor)*

Turtle: There now. I believe that will work—Neighbor.

Rabbit: I believe that's got it, Neighbor. Come on over and split a lettuce leaf with me. *(They exit together)*

An R.A. Meeting*

by Sarah Walton Miller

Prunella, Wilbur

(Small, stuffed animal sits near stage)
Prunella: Wilbur! Hey, Wilbur! Come on out and play!
(Wilbur enters)
Wilbur: Hi, Prunella.
Prunella: Hi, Wilbur.
Wilbur: I can't play.
Prunella: Why not?
Wilbur: Because.
Prunella: Because why?
Wilbur: Because I'm going to R.A.
Prunella: *(Disgusted)* An old R.A. meeting? Why?
Wilbur: We're making an African village.
Prunella: *(Surprised)* An African village?
Wilbur: *(Impatiently)* Not a real one! . . . A model
—just like a real one.
Prunella: Oh, hey, that's neat!
Wilbur: I'm making the chief's hut.
Prunella: How do you know how?
Wilbur: From books of course! We're studying Africa. It's kinda fun.
Prunella: It is?
Wilbur: It really is. Everything there is so different from here. And the missionaries help the people and everything. I like to study about something different.
Prunella: I guess. Well, if you can't play, Wilbur, I'll find somebody else . . . Hey, isn't that one of the new kids who moved in next door? That one over there? I'll go ask *him* to play!
Wilbur: No, Prunella! Don't!
Prunella: Why not?
Wilbur: You don't want to get mixed up with *him.*
Prunella: Why not?
Wilbur: Look at him. He's not like us. He's different!
(They exit)
(Follow this by letting the children, in small groups, talk about what they saw. Give them the following questions)
1. Why didn't Wilbur like the new neighbor?
2. Did you ever hear a grown-up say he didn't like someone because he's different?
3. Did you ever say it?
4. Is this a good reason for not liking? Why?

---

*Indoor/Outdoor Recreation Pack. Nashville: Broadman Press, 1976.

Do We Really Forgive?

by Sarah Walton Miller

One, Two, Three

Required: three female puppets, two of which are ugly. This skit is based on Galatians 6:1 and is especially suitable for adult Bible classes. After the presentation, let the people gather in groups of four or five and discuss in depth the question, "Do we Christians really forgive when we say we do?"
(Puppet One appears, followed by Two)
Two: Hi, there. Where are you going?
One: I'm on my way to see the pastor. *(Puppet Three appears)*
Three: Well, hello! What are you two up to?
Two: She's on her way to see the pastor.
Three: Oh? Is anything wrong?
One: Oh, no. I just want to get his permission to ask Hallie
Orpheum to work in the fifteen-year department.
Two: *(Shocked)* My dear! You *must not!*
Three: No, indeed.
Two: *(Scandalized) That* woman?
Three: Our impressionable young fifteen-year-olds?
One: *(Puzzled)* What's the matter with you? Hallie Orpheum is capable, intelligent, and charming. She loves young people and they take to her.
Three: *(Disdainfully)* Hmph! What do they know?
One: What's more, she's a dedicated Christian.
Two: *(Sniffs)* Hmph! Once tarred, always marred!
One: What?
Two: Once tarred, always marred, I said.
One: What do you mean?

31

Three: Go on—tell her.

Two: *(Self-righteously)* I don't gossip!

Three: *(Also self-righteously)* Well I certainly don't either. But she has to *know*.

Two: I guess so. You tell her.

Three? Well! Hallie Orpheum ran away with the husband of another woman in this church!

One: I don't believe it!

Two: It's true! Oh, she came back the very next day, crying and sorry. But the damage was done.

Three: The other wife got a divorce! *(In a shocked voice)* She went to *California* and married a *Methodist! (or any denomination not yours)*

One: How awful! What happened then?

Two: Then Hallie came before the whole church and asked us to forgive her! Oh, my!

Three: I tell you that was some day. Her poor husband standing right there!

Two: *(Piously)* We had to forgive her.

One: When did all this happen? Recently?

Three: Oh, no. About fourteen or fifteen years ago, wasn't it? Long before your time.

Two: Hallie was eighteen then. I remember. She married at sixteen and her husband is a lot older.

Three: *(Primly)* He was a successful, busy man!

One: Too busy, perhaps?

Three: Her Denny was in my eight-year class a few years ago.

Two: *(Grudgingly)* Those two boys turned out all right.

Three: *(Grudgingly)* Yes. At least she raised them right.

Two: Probably like their father.

One: Let me get this straight. You say you forgave her?

Two: *(Self-righteously)* Of course we did! You don't think we are unchristian, do you?

One: Good! Then I'll go see the pastor!

Three: I hope he says no.

Two: *(Urgently)* We better tell *him*.

Three: That's right. We must protect our young people.

One: You mean he doesn't know that story? How many *do* know?

Two: Oh, the older adults at least.

One: *(Thoughtfully)* I wonder—I wonder how many of *them* have secrets you wouldn't forgive either? If you knew them, that is.

Three: *(Indignantly)* Well, that's a fine attitude to take! I *told* you we forgave her!

One: Did you? *(One leaves)*

Two: Quick! Let's go around to the back—get to the pastor first! *(Two and Three leave)*

Be Patient Toward All*

by Tom deGraaf

Sally, Dad

Dad: *(Enters with new fishing pole. Flexing it. Admiring it)* What a Beauty! I'll bet she'll catch twice as many fish as my old pole . . . (Flexes pole. Looks closely at it. Lets go. It comes back and konks him) . . . Ooowee!

Sally: *(Comes up, steaming mad. Stops. Cuts loose with a terrible yell)* Yeeeahhh!!!

Dad: *(Jarred out of his senses by Sally's yell. Falls down behind the stage)*

Sally: *(Looks over to where Dad has fallen)* You OK, Dadsy?

Dad: *(Comes up on the opposite side, behind Sally)* Yes!

Sally: *(Jumps)* Don't scare me like that!

Dad: *(Bewildered)* Me scare you? That yell of yours nearly put a cardiac arrest on me.

Sally: *(Pouts)* I'm in a bad mood. Cool Charlie called me a name, and if I ever see him again it's going to be too soon! . . . I've told him five times this week not to call me names, and he still does it . . . That turkey face!

Dad: Now just calm down Sally. Cool Charlie is just teasing you—He doesn't really mean to hurt your feelings. He's just growing up and is going through a stage in his life where he thinks it's cute to call you names . . .

Sally: . . . He's about as cute as a three-legged salamander . . .

Dad: That's not nice Sally. Salamanders have nothing against you, do they?

Sally: No . . . I'm sorry.

Dad: You're just going to have to be patient with Cool Charlie. He'll grow up some day and then he won't call you names anymore.

Sally: He'd better grow up, that mealy-mouthed br . . .

Dad: (Interrupts) . . . Sally! I think you have the same thing that Cool Charlie has. Now you need to be patient with him, and I know a Bible verse that can help. Would you like to hear it?

Sally: Yes, Dad. (Sees fishing pole) Can I look at your new pole while you're telling it to me? (Takes pole—starts flexing it)

Dad: The Bible verse is First Thessalonians, chapter 5, verse 14. "Be patient toward all"—(He repeats, with more emphasis) "Be patient toward all."

Sally: (Looks at Dad) Yeah, I guess I do need to learn that verse before I smack Cool Charlie!

(She recites the verse several times—gets the audience to recite it also several times with her)

Well, thanks for that verse Dad. I think it's going to help me a lot! (She inadvertantly wacks the fishing pole down on the stage and breaks it in half) . . . Ôoops . . .

Dad: (Grabs his head in horror shakes with quiet rage) Sssaaaalllllyyy . . . You broke my new fishing pole . . .

Sally: (Hesitantly goes over to Dad and puts her arm around his neck) . . . UII, Dadsy . . . How would you like to hear a GREAT Bible verse about pa . . . (She cuts off on her word patient) . . . Maybe some other time huh . . . Gotta go—Bye Dad! (She rushes off—Comes back and sticks the busted pole into Dad's hand)

Dad: (Still livid) 8 . . . 9 . . . 10 . . . 12 . . . 13 . . . Waaaahhh! (Keels over backward)

God Is So Good

by Veteria and Derrell Billingsley

Lisa, Curt

Lisa: (Sighing and moaning) Ooh me!

Curt: (Enters, humming "God Is So Good") Hi! What's up?

Lisa: Nothing. Ooh me. (Sighs again and hangs head)

Curt: Something's wrong. What's with you?

Lisa: Oh,—nothing's wrong—and nothing's right. You just can't depend on anybody anymore.

Curt: What do you mean? I don't understand.

Lisa: Well, Greta promised to play with me this afternoon.

Curt: And?

Lisa: She went to play with Connie instead.

Curt: (Brightly) I'm here!

Lisa: Ooh! You can't play dolls!

Curt: That's your problem. You are sad because Greta broke her promise.

Lisa: I guess that's about it. Greta just doesn't like me anymore. *Nobody loves me!*

Curt: Come now. God loves you.

Lisa: So?

Curt: He will never leave you.

Lisa: How do you know?

Curt: He promised! And he never breaks a promise. You can count on that! His love is always and forever. Whether we are good or bad makes no difference—He loves us anyway.

Lisa: Yeah, (As if talking to herself) Silly me! I forgot.

Curt: Anyway, it's just like Paul said.

Lisa: Yeah? What did Paul say?

Curt: "If God be for us, who can be against us?"

Lisa: (Brightening) Oh yeah!

Curt: (Calls organist by name), play "God Is So Good" for us to sing. And "He Never Fails"—

Lisa: (Interrupting) Come on, everybody! Sing!

The Man Who Remembered

by Don Blackley

One, Two

(Characters sing first half of "Thank You for Doing It So Well" from Step Into the Sunshine, Word Records.)

One: Today we're going to talk about the Scripture, Psalm 103:1 "All that is within me, bless his holy name." But first I want *(name of child present)* to come blow this whistle. *(Child blows whistle)* That's great. Now I want you to blow it again. This time with all your might! *(Child blows whistle)* Wonderful!

Two: Now I would like for *(another child)* to get up and run around the entire circle of the children here. Start at the corner of this theatre and run clear around the group and back to the corner. Go! *(child runs)* Now *(name)* I want you to run in the same circle, but this time I want you to run as fast as you possibly can. *(Child runs)* That's great. Let's give him a hand. *(Applause)*

One: In Psalm 103 King David told himself to "Bless the Lord, O my soul, and all that is within me, bless his holy name." He told himself to bless God with everything in him.

Two: When *(name)* blew the whistle the last time, he *(she)* blew it with all his *(her)* might. When *(name)* ran around the circle the last time, he ran with all his might, as fast as he could. That's the way David said to thank God—with all your might.

One: When someone gives me a cookie I say thank you. But when someone gives me a whole plate of steaming hot cookies with chocolate on top, I get so excited and say "Oh thank you, thank you very much. Oh these are so good, thanks a lot." I get so excited!

Two: In the story today we learned about ten men who were healed of a terrible disease by Jesus Christ. Of those ten, only one remembered to come back and thank Jesus. Don't you imagine he thanked God with all his might?

One: Some people thank God a little now and then for things he gives them, but those who remember how he saved them and how he forgives their sin and is good to them every day, they want to thank him with everything that's in them.

(Name of leader) would you lead us in a prayer thanking God for all he's done for us?

(After prayer, characters sing rest of "Thank You for Doing It So Well")

The Adopted Son

by Don Blackley

Storyteller, King, Son, Boy

Storyteller: Once upon a time, many years ago, a king's son came riding down the street on a beautiful gray horse his father had given him as a birthday present.

Son: You beautiful horse. We'll have so much fun together. You're still a little wild, but we'll take care of that.

Storyteller: Suddenly, a wagon passing by them lost a wheel and crashed to the ground, frightening the beautiful horse. It began running and plunging.

Son: Whoa fellow, whoa. Settle down.

Storyteller: Suddenly the little prince saw that a small boy was standing in the path of the horse and was too scared by the large beast to move. In a flash the young prince jumped from the horse, knocking the boy out of the path of the flashing hooves. But the horse's hooves came down on the little prince instead and he lay there dead. *(Horse bounds off, little boy exits, and king enters and takes the body of son)* I suppose you might think that the king was very angry with the boy who caused the death of his son, but instead he sorrowfully sent for the boy.

King: *(Boy enters)* My boy we are very sad here in the palace because my son had to die. But we want you to come and become my son, to become the brother of my son who is dead. Although now you are very poor, because you will be my son, everything that belongs to me becomes yours. Because you will become my son, I will love you just like I loved my son that is dead.

Boy: Thank you. I'm sorry that your son had to lose his life in order to save mine. But because he loved me and was willing to die for me, I will love you and become your son. And because you have shown your great love for me, I will obey you and do whatever you command.

Storyteller: The king adopted the little boy and he became a part of the royal family. *(Characters exit except storyteller)* This is just a little picture of what Jesus Christ has done for us. When we were helpless, he came and died for us. When he was raised from the dead. Because of what Jesus did, we can become part of God's family. We do that by receiving Jesus Christ in our hearts, confessing our sin, and making God the boss of our lives. Then, like that poor little boy, we can be adopted into a royal family, the family of God.

Using Our Abilities

by Don Blackley

Farmer, Rooster, Dog, Cow

Farmer: *(Singing)* Old McDonald had a farm, E-I, E-I, O. And on this farm . . . *(Animals enter)*

Rooster: Farmer Freddie, this is a committee of all the animals on the farm. We're tired of being used and taken advantage of.

Farmer: What's this? Taken advantage of?

Dog: That's right! For years I've been looking after those silly sheep. I run all over the pasture and poop myself out keeping them out of danger. The minute I get one of them away from falling in the river I have to run over and chase another away from the barbed wire. I've had it. No more running for me. From now on it's sleeping under the porch and resting under the pecan tree.

Farmer: Oh, I see. I didn't realize you felt like you were being abused.

Cow: Well I'm abused too. Every morning and evening just as I find some wonderful green grass to graze in, I have to head back to the barn and give my milk to you.

Farmer: Let me tell you something Clarabelle. You don't give that milk, I have to take every drop of it.

Cow: Well anyway, it's just too much trouble having to drop what I'm chewing to come go through that pulling and squeezing routine. I'm through. Just chalk my name off the butterfat roster.

Farmer: OK, OK, Rooster, What's your big gripe?

Rooster? Every day since I was a young cock I've had to be the first one off that warm roost. I have to find the energy at six o'clock in the morning to flap up on a high point and crow my beak off. I'm tired of being a glorified alarm clock for this bunch of beasts.

Farmer: You're really serious about this, huh?

Rooster: I sure am. For one morning I'd like to stay cuddled up on that roost just as long as I pleased.

Farmer: OK, you're going to get that chance. Here's what I want you to do. For one month I don't want you to crawl off that roost until eleven o'clock every morning. I also don't want to hear your crowing around here during any other part of the day. If rest is what you want, that's what you'll get. Let the other roosters take care of the whole flock.

Rooster: Great! You'll not hear a sound out of me.

Farmer: Now Miss Clarabelle, I don't expect to see you around that milking barn for one month. Let the rest of the cows traipse back there every morning and evening, but I want you to stay out, and eat that lovely grass and just enjoy yourself.

Cow: With pleasure. No more cold, icy fingers for me!

Farmer: And as for you my doggy friend, I just want you

35

to lay around the house. Even if you see something that must be done with the sheep, I forbid you to take care of them for a month. Let the other dogs take care of all their problems.

Dog: Whoopee! It's cool shade and easy living for me!

Farmer: At the end of one month I'll expect to see you all back here, and not before. *(They all exit) (Farmer enters)*

Farmer: *(Whistles for the dog)* Come on over here Shep! *(Dog enters very slowly)* All right Clarabelle, it's time. *(Cow enters with her head hung low)* Where's that cocky rooster?

Rooster: *(Whispers in husky voice)* I'm coming, I'm coming!

Farmer: Well now, isn't this a happy looking bunch? *(They all shake their heads)* What? Where's all the smiles? You're not having to do all those horrible things anymore.

Cow: Oh Mr. Farmer, it's terrible. For the first few days I liked not having to come in when the rest of the cows did, but now since I haven't been giving milk, I've gone dry. And now that I'd like to be doing my part, I can't. I don't have any milk to give. I feel so useless.

Rooster: The first few days were nice, but then I started waking up long before dawn. More than anything I wanted to go out and flap my wings and wake everyone up. But you had forbidden me to use my voice. Now, because I haven't used it, it's gone. I couldn't give a healthy cock-a-doodle-doo if I wanted to.

Dog: As you can see Farmer Freddie, I'm miserable too. I haven't done anything but lay around and eat and sleep. I'm so fat I can't even scoot under the porch. And the other night when the coyote was howling, I just had to lie there. I couldn't go with the other dogs to investigate. I'm so fat that my own pups can outrun me. I'm just miserable.

Farmer: I'm certainly glad to see some animals coming to their senses around here. When God made you he gave you certain abilities. He gave you your special gift so that it might be used in serving other people. He wants you to use that gift with a glad heart, and a cheerful spirit.

You've learned that if you don't use the gift in the right way, God may take it away from you. Perhaps if you really want to be useful to God again, he will let you have your ability back.

Rooster, starting tomorrow morning I want you up using what you have left of your voice to alert the farm to a new day.

Rooster: Yessir! *(He exits)*

Farmer: Sheppy, my old friend, you head for the pasture right now and find the slowest sheep and take care of him. You have to start somewhere.

Dog: I'm on my way! *(He exits)*

Farmer: And Clarabelle, when you have your calf next month, perhaps God will let you start getting on the butter-fat list again.

Cow: I certainly hope so. Farmer Freddie I think we've all learned a big lesson about using the abilities God gives us. *(They exit)*

A Play for Puppets Without Brains

by Don Phillips

Three, One, Two, Four

Three: Hello, boys and girls!

One: How many of you like to play games? If you like to play games, then hold up your hands. *(Wait for response)* Well, today we are going to play a game called "I Am Thinking."

Two: *(Laughs)* How can you think? You haven't even got a brain!

One: Well, so what? You see those kids out there? They've got brains and they're going to help us.

Three: How's that?

One: Well, here's how we'll do it—I will give clues and hints about things that God made and see who can guess it first—you see?

Two: Not really—why don't you show me?

One: OK. Here goes. I am thinking about something that God made. It is round and yellow and . . .

Three: I know! I know! It's a grapefruit!

One: No, no silly. Let me give another hint. It is far, far away!

Two: I wish *YOU* were far, far away!

One: All right—cut the wisecracks! It warms the earth and helps the plants to grow.

Three: I give up—do any of you boys and girls out there know what it is? *(Wait for response)*

One: That's right—God gave us a good gift when he gave us the sun.

Three: Let's do another one. I am thinking about something God made. It is blue, flies, and . . .

Two: *(Very dramatic)* SUPERMAN!

Three: No, silly, let me start again. It is blue, flies, and lives in a tree.

One: Do any of you know what it is? *(Wait for response)* That's right. It's a bluebird.

Four: Can I join in? I am thinking of something that God made. It barks and wags its tail and comes in many different colors and sizes.

Two: That's easy! It's a cat!!

Four: How silly can you be? Is it a cat, boys and girls? *(Responsé)* One of you tell him what it is. *(Wait for response)* Of course, it's a dog.

One: I am thinking of something that God made. It is white and fluffy and covers the ground in the wintertime when it's real cold in some parts of the country. Boys and girls can go out and ride their sleds and play in it. Who knows what this is? *(Wait for response)* That's right—snow!

Three: Let me try it again. I am thinking of something that God made. It has on a _____ shirt *(or blouse)* *(Describe someone in the room)* and is wearing _____ . It has _____ hair.

Two: It's *ME!* IT's *ME!*

Three: Silly! You don't have _____ . *(Something different than what you described)*

One: Do any of you boys and girls know what this is? *(Wait for response)* That's right—it's _____ *(first name of person that was described)*.

Four: I am thinking of something that God made. It grows in the summer and is yellow and . . .

Two: The sun!

Four: That's not right, is it, boys and girls? The sun

doesn't shine just in the summer. What I am thinking about is good to eat and grows on a big stalk.

Three: Do any of you boys and girls know what this is? *(Wait for response)*

Four: That's right—corn!

Three: I am thinking about something God made. They come out and shine in the night and twinkle—they are far away.

One: Everyone knows what that is, don't you, boys and girls? *(Wait for response)* Of course, it's stars.

Two: You're going to be seeing stars if you don't stop this crazy game. All this thinking has made my brain hurt.

One: Now wait a minute. I thought you said we didn't have brains.

Two: Oh well, I can make a mistake once in a while, can't I?

Three: We all make mistakes, but God forgives us and still loves us just the same.

One: Don't you love God for making all the things we have talked about today?

Four: I sure do. But you know, we haven't talked about his best gift yet.

Two: What's that?

Four: Jesus. I am thinking about Jesus right now. He came into the world as a tiny baby. Soon, he was a big boy, just like some of these boys right here. Later, he grew to be a man. He was God's Son, and God sent him into the world to save us. He died on a cross for our sins, but overcame death and went back to be with God in heaven.

One: You learn about Jesus in your Sunday School class. *(Or at church, or whatever you want to emphasize at this point)*

Two: We sure hope all of you boys and girls come to Sunday School *(Or church, or whatever)* every Sunday and will invite all of your friends to come with you.

Three: It's time for us to go, so we'd better say good-bye.

Four: Before we go, remember boys and girls—you each are very special to God. He made you and loves you very much. We hope you have enjoyed this puppet show.

All: GOOD-BYE

The Lost Sheep Parable Retold

by Tommy Crow

Bernie, Alice, Burt, Narrator

Bernie: Baa-aa-aa. I'm a sheep if you couldn't guess. Baa-a-a.

Alice: Ber-rr-nie you shouldn't wander off in tha-aa-at direction. You know what Bur-rr-rt said, "It's dangerous!"

Bernie: Don't wor-r-rry about me. I'll be all right. I-I-I'm a big sheep now.

Alice: If something happens to you, I told you so! Burt's not going to be happy with you, if you're a ba-a-ad sheep.

Bernie: Ba-a-aa. This gra-a-ass looks good. An-nn-nd this looks goo-oo-ood. *(Exits)* Baa-a-aa. That was a cliff.

Burt: *(Offstage)* Ninety-three, ninety-four, ninety-five. . .

Alice: That's Bur-rr-rt our shepherd. *(Burt enters)*

Burt: *(Looking down)* Ninety-eight, *(Looking at Alice)* ninety-nine . . . Ninety-nine! Who's missing?

Alice: It's Bernie again. He wan-nn-nndered off. He's a ba-a-ad sheep.

Burt: Go back to the house with the rest of the sheep, while I find Bernie.

Alice: O-o-o-ka-aay. *(Exits)*

Burt: Bernie . . . Bernie . . . *(walks around)* I won't stop searching until I've found him. Bernie, where are you?

Bernie: *(Offstage)* I-I-I'm over here. I fell of-of-foff the cliff and I can't get back up.

Burt: Are you all right?

Bernie: Ye-e-ss. *(Bert goes down and comes up with Bernie)*

Burt: I hope you'll stay closer to the rest of the flock from now on. That way you won't get lost or fall over cliffs.

Bernie: I wi-l-ll.

Burt: At least you're safe and that's what's important.

Narrator: Burt, can I speak to Bernie for a few minutes.

Burt: Sure. *(To Bernie)* Make sure you come straight home!

Bernie: I pro-o-omise. *(Burt exits)*

Narrator: Bernie, why did you get lost? *(Bernie continues to talk in bleats)*

Bernie: What happened to me was what happened to another sheep that Jesus was talking about. But Jesus wasn't really talking about sheep, he was talking about people.

Narrator: What do you mean he was talking about people?

Bernie: What Jesus was saying is that people need someone to lead them or they get into trouble. They need Jesus to help them with their problems. But people are like me. They go and do what they want to do.

Narrator: Well how does a person follow Christ?

Bernie: Jesus is God's Son; and he said if you confess your sins, repent, and believe that he is God's Son, you wouldn't be lost anymore. And he would be your shepherd. You see, Jesus died on the cross so people wouldn't have to die because of what they do wrong.

Narrator: Jesus really must have loved us a lot to do that.

Bernie: He really did. Well, I've got to get back to the flock. Bye.

Narrator: Thank you for talking with me.

Bernie: Your wel-ll-come. Bye-ye-ye. *(Exits)*

(At this point the narrator may want to ask the children if they have any questions about what Bernie was saying.)

An Answer to Prayer

by Carroll Bryant Brown

Narrator, Katie, Little Rabbit, Ranger

Narrator: *(Backstage)* Once upon a time, a little girl named Katie wandered from her home into the bordering green forest. She was only going to go a little way and return back home before her mother knew she had gone. Katie became so intrigued by the trees and beautiful flowers that she forgot about the time. Suddenly it was dark, and after several attempts to find her way home she sat down and began to cry. She was lost!

Katie: *(Enters crying)* Boo-hoo; boo-hoo; boo-hoo.

(Wild animal screeches nearby—Katie shakes all over)

What was that? *Gulp!* I'm all alone. Just me and the, gulp, w-i-l-d a-n-i-m-a-l-s! Boo-hoo; boo-hoo!

Little Rabbit: Uh, little lady . . .

Katie: Who said that?

Little Rabbit: I did.

Katie: Why, you are a rabbit! I never met a rabbit that could talk. Uh . . . could you tell me how to get back home to my folks?

Little Rabbit: No, but I know where there is a nice little cottage to keep you warm. I'll lead you there and then tomorrow maybe you can find your way back home.

Katie: Gee, thanks. My name is Katie. Whew! It's getting awful cold *(Shivers).* Let's hurry. But first I'd better pray and ask God to send someone to find me. My mommy says that God will help people in trouble. *(Bows her head. Little Rabbit looks all around and up toward the sky. As Katie finishes she looks up.)* Amen. OK, Little Rabbit. Let's go.

Narrator: Little Rabbit led Katie to a nice dry little cottage and showed her how to light a small gas stove. Katie was happy to be warm, but she was so hungry. Little Rabbit knew where some nice nuts were buried. Katie reluctantly left her nice, warm shelter and followed Little Rabbit into the dark, cold night. While they were gone, the little cottage caught on fire. Smoke and flames could be seen for miles. Katie and Little Rabbit saw the flames and ran back.

Katie: Oh, no! My only shelter! Boo-hoo, Boo-hoo! Boo-hoo, boo-hoo. *(Little Rabbit tries to comfort her but Katie keeps crying. Little Rabbit paces back and forth. Then,* suddenly, Little Rabbit sees a forest ranger.)

Little Rabbit: Hey, Katie . . . Here comes someone to help you. Look! *(Ranger enters)*

Katie: You found me! You found me! Now I can go home to my nice bed and family. *(She runs to ranger and hugs and kisses him)*

Ranger: Yes, little girl. I saw the fire from my tower and came as fast as I could. I thought someone must be in trouble.

Katie: Well, I'll never doubt him again. No, sir-ree. *(Looks up at sky)*

Ranger: What him?

Katie: Why, God of course. I just asked him to send someone to find me and he did. Here I was feeling sorry for myself because my shelter was gone. What I thought was the worst thing that could have happened was really the best.

Ranger: Well, that's wonderful. The fire seems to have gone out. If, you're ready I'll drive you back to your home.

Katie: *(Remembers Little Rabbit)* Oh, Little Rabbit, thank you so much! I'll never forget you!

Ranger: What did you say?

Katie: I was just telling my friend, Little Rabbit, good-bye.

Ranger: Yes . . . I think it's time for one little girl to be in bed! *(Shakes head. Katie follows waving good-bye to Little Rabbit)*

The Birthday Invitation

By Veteria and Derrell Billingsley

Lucy, Mom

Lucy: Don't forget to invite Tracy to my birthday party.

Mom: OK, what about Danny?

Lucy: *(Pleadingly)* Oh, Mom! Do I have to?

Mom: *(Sternly)* And why not?

Lucy: I don't like him. He is always pulling my hair. *(Pause)* And he just *has* to be first in every game we play. Mom, he can't do anything without making a big mess! Do I have to invite him?

Mom: Lucy, perhaps Danny hasn't learned to play with other boys and girls yet. I believe that if you treat someone like you want to be treated, things will be fine.

Lucy: But Mom—he won't let anyone be nice to him. He's just mean!!

Mom: Invite him to your party. Then he will *know* that you want to be his friend.

Lucy: But why should I? I don't care if he isn't my friend!

Mom: Lucy, it is easy to be nice to those who are nice to us. Jesus wants us to be nice to everyone. This lets those who aren't so nice know that God loves them too.

Lucy: You mean that God loves Danny even though he's mean?

Mom: Yes, Lucy. God is not happy when Danny misbehaves, but he loves Danny just the same. God never stops loving us. There are times when you do not mind me, but I have never stopped loving you.

Lucy: *(Pause)* I see. *(Another pause)* Mom, let's call and invite Danny. *(Pause)* Right now! I just know that it will make him happy.

Mom: Yes. And God will be happy, too.

A Story About Jesus

by Joan King

Quacker, Mother

Quacker: *(To audience)* Mother, what are all of those people doing out there?

Mother: Well, Quacker, all of those people have come here to learn about Jesus.

Quacker: Who is Jesus, Mother?

Mother: Jesus is a man who was born in an obscure village, the child of a peasant woman. He grew up in another obscure village. He worked in a carpenter shop until he was thirty. For three years he was a preacher. He never wrote a book. He never held an office. He never owned a home. He never set foot inside a big city. He never traveled two hundred miles from the place where he was born. He had no credentials but . . . himself.

Quacker: Why would so many people want to listen to such a man, Mother?

Mother: Because, Son, of what was going to happen in a very short time in Jerusalem. Jesus, while still a young man, would have the tide of popular opinion turn against him. His friends would run away. One would deny him. He would be turned over to his enemies. He would go through the mockery of a trial. He would be nailed upon a cross between two thieves. Nineteen centuries have come and gone. Yet, he is still the centerpiece of the human race and the leader of progress. All the armies that will ever march, and all of the navies that will ever be built, and all of the parliaments that will ever sit, and all of the kings that will ever reign put together will not affect the life of man upon this earth as powerfully as that One Solitary Life.

Quacker: But, Mother, how can a dead man affect so many people?

Mother: A dead man can't, Son. Jesus overcame death —as no one else has ever done—for Jesus is the Son of God.

Quacker: The Son of God? Then why did he let people be so cruel to him, Mother?

Mother: Because he knew how mean the people on the earth had been and would continue to be. He knew that the Lord would demand that those people pay for their sins. He loved those people so much that he became a man to pay for the sins of all of those people by dying on a cross at Calvary. He overcame death so that those people can have eternal life.

Quacker: How can they have eternal life, Mother?

Mother: By faith in Jesus as the Son of God. By asking the Lord to forgive them of all of the evil things that they have done and by putting all of their trust in Jesus. Jesus promised that if they trusted him that he would send the Lord's Holy Spirit to live with them and guide them so that they could understand God's will for their lives.

Quacker: The presence of the Lord is with us, Mother. I can feel it.

Mother: Yes, Quacker, and the presence of the Lord surrounds all of those people, too.

(Song: "Sweet Sweet Spirit")

Doing Good*

by Sarah Walton Miller

Prunella, Wilbur

Prunella: I am a nice girl. I like to go about doing *good*. I have not seen Wilbur in—oh, at least a year. I will pay him a visit in the name of the church. Oh, I'm going about doing good. I am! . . . Wilbur? WILBURRR! Are you home?

(Wilbur enters, not glad to see her)

Wilbur: What do you want, Prunella.

Prunella: *(Shocked) Wilbur!* What's *happened* to you?

Wilbur: Nothing. That's it—nothing.

Prunella: *Look* at you! Wilbur, you look—*weird!*

Wilbur: If that's all you've got to say, good-bye!

Prunella: Wait, Wilbur. What's the matter?

Wilbur: Nothing, I said.

Prunella: Don't be silly. Look at you. You never *used* to look like that?

Wilbur: Like what?

Prunella: A - a - hippie! Your *hair* and that *hat* and that *thing* you're wearing.

Wilbur: Oh, go away, Prunella! You haven't changed a bit—always criticising.

Prunella: *(Getting tearful)* That's a fine way to talk to a friend!

Wilbur: Some *friend*. Where have you been all year?

Prunella: Uh—well, *busy* . . . But we're *all* your friends at the church. I *did* come to see you today.

Wilbur: Why?

Prunella: To invite you to come back to the church, silly. The people down there are anxious to have you come.

Wilbur: How anxious?

Prunella: Oh, Wilbur! You're just trying to be contrary!

Now why don't you put on something decent and cut your hair and come back to the church where you belong!

Wilbur: I *like* these clothes and I don't want to cut my hair and besides who cares if I come back? Nobody cares, that's who!

Prunella: *(Archly)* Wilburrrrrr! Don't you know God loves you?

Wilbur: Yes, but do you, Prunella? That's the really important question: do you? . . . Good-bye! *(Exits)*

Prunella: *(After a moment)* . . . Oh, well, you just can't do good by some people! Oh, I'm going about doing good, I am! *(Exits singing)*

Indoor/Outdoor Recreation Pack. Nashville: Broadman Press, 1976.

Moses

by Joyce Michaelides

One, Two

One: Hi everyone! My name is SALLY and this is my first day in Children's worship. What's your name? *(Pause for responses)* Why did you come to Children's worship today? *(Pause for responses)* Let me tell you why *I* came. I've been talking with your teacher, and he told me about all the exciting things you're going to be talking about for the next few weeks.

Two: *(Enters at the side and listens in astonishment to the things One begins to say)*

One: ———— said that you would be talking about burning bushes that don't burn up, and a large sea that parts right down the middle if you want to go through, and water that turns into *blood,* and—

Two: Hey, wait a minute! Hold on there!

One: Who are you?

Two: This is *my* first day in Children's worship, too, and I thought we were going to learn about the *Bible*.

One: Well, that's what I'm talking about—some of the exciting things that happened in the Bible.

Two: Aw, come on! You're getting mixed up with that science fiction movie that was on television last night.

One: I am not! Everything I told you about can be found in Exodus, the second book of the Bible.

Two: Oh yeah? I'm going to check that out right now! *(Starts to leave)* Uh, by the way, how do you spell Exodus?

One: Boy, what a dummy! Don't you even know how to read?

Two: I'm not a dummy! I can't read because I'm only six years old!

One: Oh! Well, you really don't have to know how to read to find out about all those exciting things I was telling you about, 'cause ———— will be teaching you all about them for the next few weeks.

Two: You mean, if I come to Children's worship for the next few weeks, I'll learn all about burning bushes that don't burn up, and a large sea that parts right down the middle if you want to go through, and water that turns into *blood,* and—

One: Yeah, that's right.

Two: Wow! I'm going to go get some of my friends and tell them about Children's worship. I bet they'd like to hear about all those exciting things, too. *(Starts to leave)*

One: You might tell them that all those things happened to a man named Moses.

Two: Who?

One: You mean you've never heard of *Moses*?

Two: No, I don't think so.

One: Boy, are you a dummy!

Two: I'm not a dummy! *(Both continue to argue as they exit.)*

The Prodigal Son

by Sarah Walton Miller

John, Reuben, Father, Mother

FOR CHILDREN

(All four puppets enter)

John: I am the Prodigal Son. They call me John. I went away from our farm.

Reuben: I am his older brother. I stayed to work the farm and make things grow.

Father: I am their father. I love both my sons.

Mother: Oh, dear! *He* let that young boy have a lot of money and let him go off to that wicked city! I said, "Don't!" I'm his mother but nobody listened to me. "He'll get into trouble!" I told my husband.

Father: She told me. And told me.

John: And she was right. I did get into trouble. I thought I was *so smart*. Smarter than my mother and my father. I was wrong. The bad people I met in the city took my money away from me. I was so silly I nearly starved to death before I came to my senses. Then I knew I wanted to go home.

Mother: Son, I'm glad you did.

John: I was afraid Father wouldn't let me come back.

Father: Son, how can you say that? We love you and we forgave you.

Reuben: *(Crossly)* I don't know about that! What about *me?* I didn't go off and waste money and get into trouble!

Father: That's right. You stayed here and took care of the farm. We love you for that. So let's all forgive John and help him once more to be one of the family.

Reuben: Well, I don't know about that.

Mother: He's your *brother*.

Reuben: That's true. It won't help to stay angry with him, will it? Then—I will forgive him, too.

John: Thank you, Reuben! Oh, thank you!

Mother: Come. Let's all go in to supper. *(They all leave)*

FOR YOUTH AND ADULTS

(Reuben enters)

Reuben: You've all heard about my brother John. The Prodigal Son, he's called. The *wastrel* son, is more like it! I'm his older brother, Reuben. A bigger piece of foolishness I've never seen. What can have possessed our father? Giving that irresponsible boy all that money and letting him go off on his own. He's back now. Whatever he got into must have been *pretty bad*. He looks as if he's been through a lot. My point is: everyone's heard of *John*. But does anyone ever hear about *me*? Did *I* waste all that money and mess my life all up? But who talks about that. *(Mother enters, calling)*

Mother: Reuben! Reuben!—oh, there you are. Your father wants you to show John over the farm today. He needs to see all the improvements made while he was—away.

Reuben: Improvements *I* made! Don't forget that: *I* made!

Mother: Of course. But John has to know if he's to share in the work.

Reuben: And in the profits, too, I suppose?

Mother: Nobody works for nothing, Reuben.

Reuben: Why can't he work to pay back all he's wasted?

Mother: *(Reproachfully)* Oh, Reuben! Shame!

Reuben: *(Forcefully)* It's not fair! It's just *not fair!* *(Father enters with John)*

Father: Oh, there you are, Reuben. I want you to show John—

Mother: *(Interrupting)* I told him already. I don't think Reuben is willing.

Reuben: I'm not! Who was it who took half our money and wasted it?

John: *(Sadly)* I did, Reuben.

Reuben: *(Angrily)* Well, it sure wasn't me! What did you do with it all? Just what have you got to show for it?

John: *(Sadly)* Nothing. Reuben, you must despise me. I'm sorry!

Mother: Oh, Reuben, can't you see that he's sorry? Your father and I forgave him. Why can't you?

Reuben: It isn't fair! Here he comes back and we're to go on as if nothing has happened. But it did happen! And *John* did it. *Not me!*

Father: No, not you, Reuben. You have always been a dependable son. I am proud of you.

Reuben: You never said so!

Father: Then I must be forgiven for that. But, Reuben, if you had been the one instead of John—don't you know we'd have forgiven you, too?

Mother: Of course, Reuben. But it was John. He's your brother, Reuben. Can't you forgive him?

Reuben: *(Grudgingly)* I suppose—if we are to work together—I'll have to forgive him. All right. I'll try.

Mother: Thank you, son. Now, Father, come with me and let the boys talk it out between them.
Father: All right, Mother. Boys, this is a happy day for us. *(Mother and Father leave)*
John: *(Ruefully)* Thank you, Reuben. I'll I'll do everything I can to deserve this chance. One day you may *really* forgive me.
Reuben: *(Grudgingly)* I guess, if I were honest—part of my resentment is that you've been places I haven't been and done things I don't even know about!
John: I pray you never do!
Reuben: *(Shyly but eagerly)* John, sometime will you tell me just what *did* happen?
John: *(Ruefully)* Reuben, you wouldn't *believe*! Well, all right. First thing, right off, when I got there—there was . . . *(They leave)*

Sally Talks to the Children*

by Tom deGraaf

Sally

Sally: *(Enters holding a daisy flower. Is very sweet)* Hi everyone. My name is Sally, and I have a very special story to tell you. It's my favorite story and I have to tell it to my friends. You're my friends, and so I'm going to tell you my story—my very special story.

Once upon a time there lived a man called Naaman. Naaman was a captain in the Army of Syria, and was a hero because he had won many important battles. Naaman had everything he could want, and was very happy.

One day something terrible happened to Naaman. Something that took away his happiness. Naaman discovered that he had gotten a disease that just could not be healed. It was the most dreaded disease in the land. It was called leprosy. Naaman knew he would die soon, and he was greatly saddened, for he was still young and had many friends.

In Naaman's house there also lived a young servant girl. She too was very sad to see Naaman slowly dying, but she knew that God could help Naaman. This little servant girl knew of a man named Elisha who could heal Naaman. Elisha was a man to whom God had given the power of healing. Elisha was the only man who could save Naaman's life.

The little servant girl summoned all her courage and told Naaman's wife that Elisha could heal him. Naaman's wife told Naaman that his only chance to be healed was to go to Elisha. So Naaman went.

Elisha was a poor man, but God loved him and gave him the wonderful power of healing. When Naaman came to see Elisha, Elisha told him that he must go and wash seven times in the Jordan River, and that he would be healed. Naaman didn't believe Elisha. How could just washing in a river heal a person of a deadly disease?

Well, after a while, Naaman finally went down and washed in the river: once, twice, three times, four times, five times, and six times. But still each time he had washed, nothing had happened. He began to doubt Elisha again, but he decided to finish what he had started and washed again a seventh time in the river.

When Naaman came up out of the water the seventh time, he could not believe his eyes! His disease had completely disappeared. He was healed! Naaman shouted for joy!

Naaman's life had been saved by Elisha's healing power! Elisha thanked God for giving him such a wonderful power. And God was pleased that the little servant girl had cared for Naaman, for it was the little girl who was really the one that helped Naaman be healed.

Have you ever tried to help someone who was sick or in trouble? The little servant girl helped Naaman by telling him where he could find help. Maybe you can tell someone that you'd like to help them when they feel bad. I try to help people as much as I can and you should too.

Does anyone here have someone in their family who is sick today? If you do, ask your mom or dad what you could do to make them feel a little better. I'm going to give my sick friend this pretty daisy because daisies are her favorite flower and they always make her feel better. She's my friend, and all of you are my friends. That means we all must help each other. Right? Right!!

I have to go now, but you remember what we talked about—Help your friends when they are sick or very sad. God is happy when you do that. And you'll be happy too. Bye-bye.

Power for Living

by Tommy Crow

Marcus, Vesta, Ben

Vesta: Have you read the ROME TRIBUNE yet?

Marcus: Not yet. Why?

Vesta: Well, you won't believe what they are saying about those Christians?

Marcus: Christians?

Vesta: You know who I'm talking about. They're the ones who follow that man from Galilee, Jesus. It's all in the paper.

Marcus: Let me see the paper. Look at what they're saying about this thing called the Holy Spirit. They say it fills you?

Vesta: It says that it happened even at what they called "Pentecost." Some said that fire was even above their heads.

Marcus: What did the governor say?

Vesta: He doesn't know what's going on.

Marcus: Look! They've got an interview with one of the people who was there! They started talking in other languages. The apostles were preaching about Jesus and they said that this man Jesus was raised from the dead. Imagine that! Someone actually coming back from the dead!

Vesta: I didn't read that part. What else does it say?

Marcus: He claims to be the only Son of the only God.

Vesta: Let's go find Ben. He can probably tell us more about Jesus since he's from Jerusalem.

Marcus: That's a good idea. *(Ben enters)*

Vesta: Ben! Ben! I'm glad we found you. I want to ask you a question.

Ben: What is it?

Vesta: Well, Marcus and I were reading the ROME TRIBUNE, and there was an article about a man from Jerusalem and the people that followed him, the Christians. We were wanting to know if you knew anything about him?

Ben: When I was in Galilee I heard him preach at one of the synagogues. He claimed to be the Son of the one and only true God. And he is! The Roman soldiers put him to death on a cross outside of Jerusalem, and three days after he died he came back to life! There were soldiers guarding his grave and they said that an angel rolled away the boulder that was covering the mouth of his grave and he walked out alive!

Marcus: Wow! That's almost too good to be true.

Ben: But it is true.

Vesta: But what does that have to do with this Holy Spirit?

Ben: When Jesus had to go back to heaven to be with God, he promised to send back the Holy Spirit to those who are Christians. It is this Spirit that helps Christians know when they are following God and when they are not.

Vesta: How do you become a Christian?

Ben: Jesus said that you must confess your sins, repent, and believe in your heart that Jesus is the Son of God. The Holy Spirit will come into your life and give you strength to share your witness with others and to endure rough times.

Vesta: I believe in my heart that Jesus is the Son of God and that he died for what I have done wrong.

Marcus: Is the Holy Spirit with her?

Ben: Yes he is.

Marcus: Then how come I can't see him?

Ben: Because he is invisible.

Marcus: I want to become a Christian too.

Ben: Of course you know what the cost of becoming a Christian is?

Marcus: I know, but Vesta looks so peaceful and happy. That's what I want.

Ben: You've just got to ask him in and then the Holy Spirit is with you.

Marcus: I know God will protect us through his Holy Spirit.

Free, Yet Accountable*

by Frank Hart Smith

Two boy puppets, three girl puppets

B-One: Eve.

G-Three: And Adam.

B-Two: I never heard it in that order before, but it's just as exciting that way. And it must have been exciting in that garden . . . er, what was its name?

G-Two: Eden, you dummy. You'd forget your own name if it weren't sewed in the lining of your jacket!

B-Two: Yeah, Eden. They really had it good. When I think of all the lawns I had to mow this past summer, and when I . . .

G-Three: Just a minute, what about all my hours of horror working at the store? Those old ladies are terrors during the sales. Wow, could I use a Garden of Eden!

B-One: I think the greatest thing about the place was that they didn't have a mom and dad yelling at them all the time.

G-Three: Or brothers and sisters driving them out of their mind.

G-One: I don't know, they had it good, but something happened. They had freedom but they goofed it up.

All B: Goofed is right.

All G: And I suppose you two think it was all her fault?

B-One: Well, she did get involved in conversation with the serpent.

G-Two: And I suppose you think she said,

G-Three: "The devil made me do it!"

All G: And that was that!

G-One: Well, there was more to it than that, and we need to look at sin as hard as they did.

All B: Sin, that's kinda hard for us to face up to, don't you think?

G-One: Well, if I read Genesis and Galatians and a few passages in between right, you've got to face up to it.

G-Two: All that fruit, and they wanted the one they couldn't have.

B-Two: Huh?

G-Two: I mean, they had it so good, why goof it all up?

G-One: Can't you look at us and see us doing the same thing? We really have it pretty good, but lots of times we goof it up by wanting just the thing that's not good for us.

B-One: You're preaching now, sister. You are kidding, aren't you?

G-One: Friend, I'm serious.

All G: Serious.

All B: Serious.

All: Serious!

B-One: O.K., I see what you mean. But what does it mean to have your own little Garden of Eden? Is that what it means to be free?

G-One: Free, now there is a key word.

All G: Free—the key.

All B: Free—the key.

All: Free—the key.

B-Two: Free—does that mean free to do just anything as long as it doesn't hurt someone else?

B-One: I don't know, that just sounds like too much rationalizing.

G-One: That's a mighty big word, but I know what it means because I'm the world's authority on the subject. So we rationalize by making freedom mean I can do my thing.

G-Two: I think free means more—like free not to do wrong. That's a backdoor approach, but I think doing wrong ties you up.

All B: Yeah, ties you up.

All G: Ties you up.

All: And—ties you down . . .

B-One: Cause when you're tied down, you can't

B-Two: Soar!

All: Yeah!

G-Three: You said "free" meant being free not to do wrong, a backdoor approach. What's the front way?

B-One: The front way has gotta be his. He says it means being free to

G-One: Love!

B-Two: Care!

G-Two: Share!

All B: And Serve?

All G: Serve? Like to help? Like with the dishes?

All: Ohhhhhhhhhhhhhhhhhhh!

B-One: And you know what else it means?

G-Three: Nope.

B-One: It means loving and caring and sharing with . . .

B-Two: With?

B-One: Your own brother.

All: (Groan) Ugh!!

The First People*

by Lyn Yarborough

Emcee, Adam, Eve, Snake, Voice

Emcee: Everybody shut your eyes and cover your ears and imagine what it was like before God created the earth. There was nothing to see and nothing to hear.

In the beginning, God created the heaven and the earth. He created the sun and the moon, the flowers and trees, and all the living things. Last of all, he created man and woman. *(Adam and Eve enter)*

Adam: What a beautiful world God created. Look at that flower—and the trees.

Eve: Yes, it's just beautiful. This flower smells so good. *(Sniff)*

Adam: It's a beautiful world, all right. But it sure was lonesome before God created you, Eve.

Eve: Why, Adam, that's sweet of you to say that. *(A turtle enters)*

Adam: Oh, here's an animal I haven't named yet. God told me to give a name to all the animals in the garden. Let's see, now. I think I'll call it a turplear.

Eve: I think that sounds silly. I like rootle best. He's so cute.

Adam: That's crazy. Let me think now . . . I've got it . . . let's combine turplear and rootle and you get . . .

Eve: *(Interrupts)* Rooplear.

Adam: . . . Turtle. That's what I'll call it . . . a turtle. I'd better take him back to the pond. I'll be back soon.

Eve: Don't forget.

Adam: I won't forget. I'll be back in plenty of time for us to take our evening walk with God. Come on, little turtle. *(Adam, turtle exit, snake peeks from behind tree)*

Snake: Eve.

Eve: *(Looks around)* Who's there? I thought Adam and I were the only ones around.

Snake: Hello, Eve. Here I am. This is a lovely garden you have here. Does it all belong to you?

Eve: Oh, yes. God gave it all to us.

Snake: All of it?

Eve: Well . . . . all but that tree you're standing under. We're not supposed to eat the fruit from that tree. God said we would die.

Snake: Eve . . . Eve. Surely you don't believe that. You won't die. God just told you that so you wouldn't be as smart as he is. If you would eat this fruit, you'd be just like God!

Eve: Well, I don't know. It does look good. I don't guess just a little bit would hurt. *(She takes bite. Adam enters as she takes bite, snake hides behind tree)*

Adam: What do you have there, Eve? Who was that behind the tree?

Eve: Here, Adam, this is delicious. Try it. *(Adam takes bite, they look at each other, then look around)*

Adam: Uh oh, we shouldn't have done that, Eve. Quick, we have to hide! God will be here soon. *(They hide behind bush)*

Voice: Adam. Adam. Where are you?

Adam: Here I am, Lord.

Voice: Why are you hiding, Adam?

Adam: I was ashamed, Lord.

Voice: Ashamed? Of what? Didn't I give you control of everything in the garden? Why should you be ashamed? Have you been eating the fruit of the forbidden tree?

Adam: The woman you gave me said it was good and I ate it.

Eve: Well, it's not all my fault. The serpent tricked me.

Voice: I'm sorry, Adam. You too, Eve. But now you'll have to leave the garden and never come back. Your life will be filled with hard work until the day you die. As for you, serpent, you will be hated and despised. One day, I'll put an end to you.

(Snake slinks off. Adam and Eve hang their heads and exit sadly)

Emcee: It made God sad that Adam and Eve had done wrong, but he still loved them very much. He didn't stop loving Adam and Eve, and he didn't stop loving the people who came after them. God had a plan that would let the people of the earth walk with him again. That plan was Jesus.

"For God so loved the world that he gave his only begotten son that whosoever believeth in him shall not perish, but have everlasting life" (John 3:16).

*Reprinted from *The Puppet Ministry Handbook.* © Copyright, 1974. Puppets 'n' Stuff, Dallas, Texas. Used by permission.

The One that Got Away*

by Tom deGraaf

Dad, Willie, Cool Charlie, Mom

(All enter with fishing poles, very excited.)

Willie: Oh! Wow! This is gonna be one out-a-sight fishing trip!

Charlie: You said it, Baby! Cool Charlie is going to catch the biggest trout since the rainbow Noah saw! Thanks a lot, Mr. Weekers, for inviting me to come along on a fishing trip.

Dad: Well, it was kind of a last minute deal, but I'm glad you and Willie could come. I hope you boys didn't already have something else planned.

Charlie: Oh, no. We didn't have anything else to do, did we Willie?

Willie: *(He knows they both did—but tries to cover up.)* . . . Uh . . . No . . . We didn't have anything else to do . . . not a thing. . . .

Mom: *(Offstage)* Willie! I thought you and Cool Charlie were going visiting with the Youth group from the church today?! What in the world are you doing with your fishing poles? Does your father know about this?

Willie: *(Looks at Dad—Laughs weakly.)* . . . Hee Hee . . . I guess we did have something else to do besides go fishing . . . Hee Hee . . .

Dad: *(Looks at them. They try to laugh.)* Well boys, it seems like you were trying to ditch out on going visiting with the Youth group . . . Am I correct?

Charlie: *(Scared)* . . . Seems like . . .

Dad: Here you're supposed to be going out and inviting your friends to church and, instead, you decide to go fishing! What do you have to say for yourselves?

Willie: Cool Charlie made me do it! He made me do it! *(Points at him with fishing pole.)* It's his fault!

Charlie: Me? It was your idea too you know! *(Wacks Willie with pole. They fence with their poles.)* Take that!

Dad: OK, Stop it! You're both at fault here, and I think you need to learn a lesson about doing what you're supposed to do instead of what you want to do.

Willie: Are you going to spank us? Huh, are you gonna spank us?

Dad: Well, I'm going to tell you boys a story . . . first.

Charlie: *(To Willie)* Is that better or worse?

Willie: *(To Charlie)* Worse! That means we gotta listen to the story plus get a spankin'!

Dad: Now be quiet and listen. *(Clears his throat)* This is a story from the Bible about the big one that finally got away.

Charlie: You mean a big fish got away from some guy?

Dad: I mean some guy—Jonah was his name—got away from a big fish!

Willie: Far out! A guy got away from a fish! Big deal.

Dad: Cool it Willie, this is a Bible story. Show a little reverence. Now as I was saying, Jonah was a man who disobeyed God.

Charlie: What'd he do?

Dad: God told Jonah to go to a city called Nineveh and preach. Well, Jonah didn't want to, so he ran off in the opposite direction and took a boat ride. Jonah thought that by going out in a small boat on the ocean, God wouldn't be able to find him. Fat chance! God saw Jonah out in the boat and decided to teach him a lesson. He sent a terrible storm that was about to sink Jonah's ship. All the sailors on board were scared they were all going to drown, so they began to pray. But Jonah knew that it was his fault. He knew God was angry with him, and that's why the storm had come. So Jonah told the sailors that there was only one way to be saved from drowning, and that was to throw him overboard.

Charlie: Where does the fish come in?

Dad: Right here. You see, the sailors did throw Jonah overboard, and a giant fish swallowed Jonah!

Willie: Gross!!

Dad: And the storm stopped. Well Jonah found himself sitting down in the dark belly of that fish wondering how he was ever going to come out alive! He prayed and prayed and told God that he was sorry for running away and not preach-

47

ing to Nineveh. He told God that if he could have one more chance, he would make good. Now that is exactly what God wanted to hear! After a couple more days went by and the fish got closer to land, God gave him a stomach ache so that he spit Jonah right up onto dry land!

Charlie: The fish spit him out? I'll bet that was weird!

Dad: It could have been worse. Anyway, Jonah hit the beach running. He went straight to Nineveh and the entire city was saved because of his preaching!

Willie: Hey, that's a neat story! Instead of the big fish getting away from the man, a man gets away from a big fish!

Charlie: Hey, yeah!

Dad: But the whole point of the story is that if you're supposed to do something for God, you'd better do it. And God will bless you for it. He saved the whole city of Nineveh didn't he?

Willie: Yeah . . . I guess you're right, Dad.

Charlie: You're entirely right, Mr. Weekers!

Dad: Now . . . weren't you boys supposed to go visiting people to invite them to church?

Willie: Yeah. I guess we'd better get going. We'll go fishing some other time, Dad.

Charlie: See ya later Mr. Weekers! *(Both start to exit)* . . . Uh, Mr. Weekers . . . about that spanking?

Dad: Well, I'll forget about it this time . . . *(Looks up, then at Charlie)* . . . But don't go out in any small boats!

Charlie: *(Looks up, then at Dad)* . . . Right! *(They exit.)*

---

*Adapted from *California Puppets*, Mill Valley, California. © Copyright, 1975. Used by permission.

Noah and the Ark*

by Pat Elam

Man, Noah, Shem, Narrator, Voice, Wife

(Noah, whistling and hammering)

Man: *(Enters)* Hey, Noah. That sure is a big boat. What is it for?

Noah: Oh, this is the ark. God told me to build it because he is going to send a flood to destroy the earth.

Man: You've got to be kidding. Why would God want to destroy the earth?

Noah: Because the people no longer love him. They won't do what he asks them to do and they live wicked lives. So God is going to start all over again.

Man: *(Laughing):* That's the silliest story I've ever heard. I don't believe it. Ha ha, a flood, ha ha. *(Exits, laughing)*

Noah: *(Calling after the man)* Well, it's true. God told me, and I'm going to do what he says.

Shem: *(Enters)* Dad, I've measured the ark and it's 350 feet long, 75 feet wide, and 45 feet high. Is that okay?

Noah: No, Shem. It's got to be longer. God said 450 feet long.

Shem: Well, if you say so, but we don't have any more wood.

Noah: Then we'll just have to go out and find some more. Come on now, run and get your brothers. There's still more work to be done. *(They exit)*

Narrator: So Noah and his sons and family worked until the ark was completed. It took a long time, but Noah believed God and kept on working. God would reward Noah by saving him and his family from the flood which was soon to come.

Noah: *(Enters mumbling)* Now, let me see. The boat's the right size, and the . . .

Voice: Noah *(Noah looks around, puzzled)*

Voice: Noah

Noah: Is that you again, Lord?

Voice: Yes, Noah. It's time to gather all the animals into the ark. Bring in two or more of every kind so they will be safe from the flood. In one week I will begin forty days and nights of rain, and everything on the earth will be destroyed.

Noah: Yes, Lord. I'll begin right away. *(Exits. Music plays as Noah enters, leading animals. They file by, as if entering the ark.)*

Noah: Step lively there, Mr. Turtle, we don't have all day, you know. We've got to move faster, now. Come on, now, let's don't monkey around. Here we go. Move it up, move it up. Watch your head there, Giraffes. Is everyone here? It's time to shut the door.

Narrator: When all were safely inside the ark, the Lord shut the door and the rains began. For 40 days and nights the rains came down and slowly covered the earth.

48

(Noah comes out on porch of boat under cover. Enter Shem.)

Shem: We've had a little accident, Father.

Noah: What seems to be the trouble, Son?

Shem: It seems that this little squirrel's tail is broken. The elephant stepped on it. Oh, he didn't mean to, but it is so crowded down there. And the animals are getting restless.

Noah: Yes, Son, I know. The rain will stop soon. But first, let's take care of this little fella. *(They put a splint or bandage on squirrel's tail.)* There now, you'll be better right away. *(Exit Shem and squirrel)*

Noah: The animals are getting restless. Maybe if I send out the dove again, she could find a dry place. *(Noah exits and returns with his wife.)*

Noah: I sure hope that little dove finds some sign of dry land. The raven we sent out a few days ago didn't even come back.

Wife: Oh, look, Noah! Here comes the dove now, and she's carrying an olive branch!

Noah: It won't be long now. The olive branch is a sign that dry land is nearby. Let's go and get the animals ready to leave the ark.

(Noah, wife start to exit. Shem enters excitedly. Noah turns back to Shem)

Shem: Father, Father. The ark is on dry land. The water is gone.

Noah: Good. It's time to leave the ark. We must let the animals go so they can find a new home. Let's get the family together and go build an altar on the mountain and give thanks to God. *(All exit)*

(Noah, wife enter. A rainbow rises above them)

Voice: I will not again curse the ground any more for man's sake . . . While the earth remaineth, seedtime and harvest, and cold and heat, and summer and winter, and day and night, shall not cease (Gen. 8:21-22).

A Man in God's Plan*

by Frank Hart Smith

Two boy puppets, Three girl puppets

B-One: *(Singing)* Row, row, row your ark,
    Hope it doesn't leak!
    Merrily, merrily, merrily, merrily,
    Dodge that mountain peak!

G-Two: Now there's a song if ever I heard one.

B-One: Thanks.

G-Two: I didn't say what kind of song. But now I will—it was terrible.

B-One: Thanks for nothing.

G-Two: Anyway, why were you singing that?

B-One: I've been digging deeper in Genesis, and I've come up with a flood of information.

G-Two: I can't stand it.

B-Two: I can't either, but I've always had a low toleration point for disasters.

G-Three: What I think our brother is saying is that he has been reading the story of Noah.

B-One: Give that lady a prize for her keen sense of observation.

G-One: What can you say constructive about Noah, maybe something that no one's thought of before?

B-One: Well, to begin with "constructive" is a good word to use in talking about Noah.

G-One: O Lord, help me to love him in spite of his misguided humor!

B-Two: speaking of humor, Noah must have had a real sense of it. God, too. Imagine being told to build a boat:

G-One: 450 feet long,

B-Two: 75 feet wide,

G-Two: 45 feet high!

G-Three: Not to mention the fact that it was to have

B-One: Three decks and a door!

B-Two: And all of this right in the middle of the pasture. Not an ocean for miles and miles. Noah's neighbors must have thought he was crazy.

G-One: Probably so. Wouldn't you?

B-Two: I guess I would have.

B-One: Then God told ole Noah to get his wife and his sons and their wives and to get on board.

G-Three: That wasn't all they were to get on board . . .

G-One: God said to get two of every

All B: Animal,

G-One: Two of every

All G: Bird,

G-One: And two of every

All G: *(Shivering)* Creeping thing. I wish he'd left those

49

creepy crawlies off!

B-Two: And then when all were safely on board and

G-Two: The doors were shut

G-One: And the animals and birds were making all kinds of noises

B-One: And the folks from miles around were outside laughing and hee-hawing at ole Noah . . .

All B: Then, it happened . . .

All G: It began to rain . . .

B-One: And it rained,

G-One: And it rained,

B-Two: And it rained,

G-Two: And it rained,

B-One: And it rained,

G-Three: And it rained some more.

All G: There just wasn't much left

All B: Except Noah, his family, and the animals and birds and creeping things.

B-One: And finally, when the rain was over

G-One: And the waters subsided,

All G: God did a wonderful thing—

All: He sent a rainbow . . .

G-Two: Flinging colors into the sky.

B-Two: As his promise nevermore to destroy the earth by flood.

B-One: And what does Noah have to say to us?

G-One: I think it says we should start doing what God says even when it isn't cloudy. Or even if it is.

B-Two: I think it says that God can and will use us if we're willing to listen to him instead of those around us who keep laughing at us.

G-Three: I think it means that God has something great for all of us. We just need to listen and he'll tell us:

G-One: How long,

B-One: And how wide,

G-Two: And how high,

G-Three: And anything else we need to know.

G-One: I think this roaming through Genesis has been a keen experience.

Weird Larry—the Good Samaritan*

by Tom deGraaf

Willie, Seymore, Cool Charlie, Lucy, Weird Larry

(Willie has Band-Aids all over and a black eye)

Willie: *(Enters, all beat up. Groans)* Oooo . . . Oweee . . . Man I just got beat up—BAD!! I was just walkin' along, listening to my radio (K-F-R-C) when all of a sudden, WHAM! Some turkey jumped me from behind! WOW, he put some Kung-Fu on my body and then ripped off my radio . . . I didn't even get to finish listening to my favorite song! Boy do I feel Baaaaadd . . . *(He looks around)* I sure wish somebody would come by and give me a ride home—I can hardly even walk . . .

Seymore: *(Enters)* Oooo Willie! What happened to you? You look like you got sucked up a vacuum cleaner!

Willie: I feel awful Seymore. Some turkey jumped me and took my radio—Wouldn't even let me finish my favorite song . . . Do you think you could help out and give me a ride home? I can't walk so good right now. He bruised my bunions.

Seymore: Sorry Willie, I can't. I got a heavy date with Big Bertha in a couple minutes and I gotta truck on over and pick her up. And believe me, it takes a truck to pick her up!

See ya Willie.

Willie: Aw nuts. I'm feeling really bad now. I wish somebody would give me a ride. I just gotta get home where my mom can patch me up. *(Looks down slowly, then at audience)* Oh no, my navel just sunk.

Cool Charlie: *(Enters)* Hey Willie Baby!

Willie: Cool Charlie! Oh! Wow am I glad to see you! I've been mugged! Can you please help me . . . I just gotta have a ride home.

Cool Charlie: Hey I'm really sorry man, but I can't give you a ride right now . . .

Willie: But Cool Charlie, I really need help and this could be your good deed for today . . . I thought you were a Boy Scout?

Cool Charlie: Wrong man!! I joined the Girl Scouts! I ain't got time for you man, 'cause my chicks's waiting. We're gonna go sell cookies! *(Exits)*

Willie: Wow. If I don't get help soon I'm gonna faint or something. Besides, these Band-Aids are giving me a rash!

Lucy: *(Enters, practicing cheerleading with a pompom)*

50

La-Dee-Da-Dee, La-Dee-Da . . . EEK!!! *(Looks closely at Willie)* Yuk-O! What happened Willie!? Are you selling Band-Aids or impersonating a shag rug with third-degree mothbite?!?

Willie: Oh Lucy, You're my last hope! I got mugged and I'm too beat up to walk home. Could you please give me a ride to our house so Mom can fix me up?

Lucy: Oh Willie I'm sorry, but I'm on my way to cheerleading practice. I gotta go over a few "Get it on Turlock High" yells for the game next week.

Willie: But Lucy, I got a real bad pain on my kneecap. You gotta help me!

Lucy: Sorry, Willie, but I have to go now. *(Exits doing "cheers")*

Willie: *(Slowly looks all around)* I'm doomed . . . My best friend Seymore wouldn't help me . . . And now the sweetest girl in the whole school, Lucy, hasn't got time to help me . . . I'm doomed . . . Finished . . . *(Weird Larry enters. Listens)* . . . Ka-put!

Larry: Gesundheit!!

Willie: *(Depressed)* Oh, hi Weird Larry . . .

Larry: What's the matter Willie? You're all covered with Band-Aids and you look like you just lost your best friend.

Willie: Three best friends, Larry. And I'm covered with Band-Aids because I got beat up, you nit-wit. Nobody wants to help me get home. I'm doomed.

Larry: I'll help you!

Willie: You? . . . But I didn't think we were friends. Remember last week when I smacked you in the cafeteria?

Larry: Aw, that's OK—It was my fault. I spilled my milk on your shirt. But never mind that. How can I help you, Willie?

Willie: Well, I really need a ride home 'cause I can't walk so good.

Larry: Don't worry about a thing I got my motor bike parked right outside!

Willie: *(Looks sickly at audience)* You don't mean the one with the training wheels . . .

Larry: *(Proudly)* Yep! That's the one. Let's go!

Willie: *(Seriously)* Larry—Thanks. You're sort of like the Good Samaritan aren't you . . . Helping me like this I mean. You sure are doing a nice thing for me. How can I ever thank you enough Larry ol' pal?

Larry: *(Confidently)* Uh, Willie—You'd better save your thanks until after we get to your house. *(Laughs)* You've never seen me drive a motorcycle before, have you? *(Exits)*

Willie: *(Faints)*

(Have someone recap the story, emphasizing the good deed Weird Larry was willing to do—and did do.)

---

*Reprinted from *California Puppets*, Mill Valley, California. © Copyright, 1975. Used by permission.

A Matter of Honesty*

by Sarah Walton Miller

Maid, Zenobia, Zacchaeus

Maid: *(Enters)* Once upon a time, a long time ago—that's the way good stories begin, don't they? Now our story is about a man named Zacchaeus.

Zacchaeus: *(Enters)* I'm Zacchaeus.

Maid: *(To audience)* Yes, that's Zacchaeus, all five feet of him. If he had a home, he had a family. If he had a family, it started with a wife.

Zenobia: *(Enters)* I am his wife.

Zacchaeus: Zenobia, my dear, you look lovely today.

Zenobia: Thanks to your generosity, Zacchaeus.

Maid: *(Ironically, aside to audience)* One look at *me* and you can see where his generosity stopped! I'm their maid, Hannah.

Zenobia: Zacchaeus, I'm so unhappy!

Zacchaeus: But my love, you have everything.

Maid: *(Aside)* Including him.

Zenobia: None of the other wives come to visit! And the children are *shunned* at synagogue school.

51

Zacchaeus: Tish tush! Jealousy, my dear. Jealousy of all we have.

Maid: *(Aside)* The truth is everybody hates *him*. Hobnobbing with those Romans. Taking more tax money than the law requires.

Zenobia: Zacchaeus, perhaps we shouldn't have so much—

Zacchaeus: Nonsense, my dear!

Zenobia: Or at least live more simply.

Zacchaeus: Zenobia! Feeling guilty? Someone has to do my job.

Maid: *(Aside)* He *over*does it!

Zacchaeus: If some of our people don't see it that way —well they deserve to pay more.

Zenobia: But, Zacchaeus, we live so apart—from the synagogue, except for the children. You never go to temple.

Zacchaeus: *(Loudly)* A dying institution!

Zenobia: You never give your tithes . . .

Zacchaeus: *Tithes!* A racket! Priests gouging the people!

Zenobia: But tithes and offerings *belong* to the *Lord!* It's one thing to cheat your fellowmen . . .

Zacchaeus: *(Loudly, hurt)* Zenobia!

Zenobia: But to cheat the *Lord*—oh, Zacchaeus.

Zacchaeus: *(With forced patience)* Zenobia, I should be angry with you. But I remember your frailties. After all, you are only a woman.

Maid: *(Aside, groans dramatically)* Oh, *really!*

Zacchaeus: Now, don't you worry your pretty self. How would you like a length of that sheer Egyptian linen for a scarf? There's a dealer in from Thebes. *(Zenobia, Zacchaeus exit)*

Maid: Well, there they go, my master and mistress. She really was unhappy, poor thing. Deep down inside she misses the temple.

Zenobia: *(Enters)* Hannah, are you going to the temple today?

Maid: Yes, mistress.

Zenobia: I have a bag of gold coins. Will you take them for me? Don't tell Zacchaeus!

Maid: No, mistress.

Zenobia: *(Fervently)* Oh, Hannah, if only Zacchaeus . . . *(Exits)*

Maid: Yes, mistress. *(Pause)* Well, things didn't get better because Zacchaeus didn't get better. Their oldest son was in a fight at the synagogue school—some of the children called his father names. My mistress was lonely. And my master became richer and richer. Then one day . . .

Zenobia: *(Enters, excited)* Hannah, there's a prophet from Nazareth here in the city.

Maid: Yes, mistress. Jesus is his name.

Zenobia: Hannah, I want to hear him! If we disguise ourselves . . .

Maid: *(Aside)* Oh, oh! Here comes trouble.

Zacchaeus: *(Enters)* What's this? Disguise yourselves? Why? Why?

Zenobia: *(Upset)* So no one will recognize me. Oh, Zacchaeus, I want to hear this prophet, Jesus!

Zacchaeus: Absolutely not! I forbid it!

Zenobia: Please, Zacchaeus. They say he's a great man.

Zacchaeus: Nonsense! He's a charlatan, a fraud!

Zenobia: They say he works miracles!

Zacchaeus: Impossible!

Zenobia: Zacchaeus, he's speaking in the temple!

Zacchaeus: Absurd. Who would let him? Who would listen to him?

Maid: *(Slyly)* Master, Jesus speaks often in the temple!

Zacchaeus: Be quiet, girl! A person like that? No visible means of support? If I were his tax gatherer, I'd soon see.

Zenobia: *(Ironically)* I'll bet *he* doesn't pay tithes and offerings! Think *that* over!

Zenobia: *(Upset)* Oh, but he must—surely—Hannah?

Maid: Mistress, if he *didn't*, those lawyers who are always after him, would have some *real* evidence against him! Believe me!

Zenobia: *(Triumphantly)* You see? You're just using that as an excuse. Oh, Zaccheus, forgive me! Please let me go.

Zacchaeus: *(Overdoing kindness):* My dear, you are not yourself. Come and rest awhile. *(Zenobia, Zacchaeus exit)*

Maid: No, she didn't go. *He* saw to that. Then Jesus went away.

Zenobia: *(Enters; speaks to audience)* But Jesus is coming back at last! I heard the servants talking. Oh, if only I might hear him when he comes. *(Exit)*

Zacchaeus: *(Enters, speaks to audience)* I *will not* have my family involved with this—this—oh, I know people hate me! If it weren't me, though, it would be someone else.

Maid: *(Aside)* Praise the Lord!

Zacchaeus: Who knows? Maybe the next tax collector would be very unkind! Not thoughtful and forbearing like me! *(Exits)*

Maid: *(Looks down where he left, thoughtfully—then)* He's kidding! Or, is he?

Zenobia: *(Enters after pause; excited)* Hannah! Hannah!

Maid: Yes, mistress?

Zenobia: Oh, Hannah, tell me! Hannah, have you heard? Jesus is coming back! But of course you've heard. You servants always seem to know first.

Maid: Yes, mistress.

Zenobia: When, Hannah? *When?*

Maid: Mistress, he is already here. I heard from Rachel, the maid next door. He will be passing along *our* street this afternoon!

Zenobia: *(Happily)* He *will?* Marvelous! Marvelous!

Zacchaeus: *(Enters)* Ah, my dear, you sound happy.

Maid: *(Aside)* But not for long. Now.

Zenobia: Oh, Zacchaeus! Jesus is coming!

Zacchaeus: *(Gruffly):* Not soon, I hope.

Zenobia: *(Happily)* Today, Zacchaeus! This very afternoon!

Zacchaeus: *(Sternly)* I have said my say!

Maid: *(Aside)* That he has.

Zacchaeus: You cannot go to the temple to hear this—this charlatan.

Zenobia: *(Triumphantly)* Not the temple! *Here!* On our street! Isn't it *wonderful?* *(Zenobia, Zacchaeus exit)*

Maid: Wonderful wasn't quite the word he'd have chosen. At least he didn't forbid her looking out her own window, I looked, too. Soon crowds gathered along the street, knowing Jesus was coming that way soon. Mistress! Mistress! Come quickly!

Zenobia: *(Enters, excited)* What is it, Hannah!

Maid: *(Looking)* Look down in the street!

Zenobia: Is Jesus coming?

Maid: No, look right down below the window!

Zenobia: *(Looks)* It can't be! It is! It's Zacchaeus!

Maid: Mistress, those men, I think they mean harm . . .

Zenobia: *(Calling out)* Zacchaeus! Zaccheaus, watch out!

Maid: He can't hear you, Mistress.

Zenobia: *(Gratefully)* Oh! They've turned away.

Maid: See? Because Jesus is coming down the street!

Zenobia: Look at Zacchaeus trying to get through the crowd! They won't let him. He's *so short,* poor Zacchaeus!

Maid: What's he doing? Look, Mistress, he's trying to climb that tree.

Zenobia: Oh, dear. At his age, he could fall and hurt himself.

Maid: Yes!

Zenobia: He made it! Hannah, look at the prophet! He's stopped! Is he talking to *Zacchaeus?* What's he saying? I have to hear! *(Exits)*

Maid: There's no accounting for taste. The prophet and his party came into *our* house for dinner! Well, I don't know what the magic was—but whatever it was, has lasted. It's been three months, Zacchaeus *now* is *unbelievable.* Why he's even nice to me! *(Zacchaeus, Zenobia enter)*

Zenobia: Zacchaeus, I'm so proud of you. Paying back all that money—all the things you've tried to make right.

Zacchaeus: In the eyes of some, nothing I do will ever be right.

Zenobia: Our home is different.

Maid: *(Aside)* Amen!

Zenobia: The children are happier. And I enjoy visits—well, from *some* of the wives.

Zacchaeus: Good. Good.

Zenobia: Now you go to the temple. And you always pay your tithes and take offerings with you, too.

Zacchaeus: *(Surprised)* Of course. Why not? I've always told you it's wrong for a man to try to cheat God. Zenobia, I'll have to counsel with you. Women have a strange moral sense. The feminine mind is lax in these matters. My dear, it takes a strong masculine hand to guide women!

Zenobia: *(Sighs happily)* Yes, Zacchaeus!

Maid: *(Marveling)* Isn't he *something?* You know he really *believes* all that? Oh, well, it's not important. What *is* important is that Jesus came to this house and made honor and honesty synonymous.

Alas the Poor King!

by Sarah Walton Miller

Nebuchadnezzar, Captain, Daniel, Shadrack, Meshack, Abednego, Steward

Nebuchadnezzar: *(Enters. Looks about, annoyed at lack of reception)* Well—blow the trumpets, somebody! Sound the drums! Don't you recognize a king when you see one? *(Shouts)* Let's hear it for the King! *(Applause)* That's more like it! I need all the approval I can get. Sometimes things happen to hurt a king's ego. A king can feel insecure, too. Wait till I tell you what happened to me! It shouldn't have happened to a dog, much less a king! King Nebuchadnezzar of Babylon—that's me! It all started when those people over in Jerusalem refused to pay taxes. Well, now, no self-respecting king would put up with that! I called the captain of my armies—CAPTAIN! *(Captain enters)*

Captain: Yes, Your Majesty?

Nebuchadnezzar: Assemble the armies! We march on Jerusalem! *(Kazoos play a march. The king followed by the Captain and puppet soldiers "march" across and repeat a couple of times. They withdraw. Nebuchadnezzar returns)*

Nebuchadnezzar: That was my first mistake. Any king mixing up with those Hebrews is bound to lose his dignity. *I* should have stayed home. We won, of course. Or did we? Anyway, as was the custom, I took back to Babylon the pick of the youth of Jerusalem. *(Daniel enters, followed by Shadrack, Meshack and Abednego)*

Daniel: I'm Daniel!

Nebuchadnezzar: *(Groans)* Don't *I* know!

Daniel: These are my friends—Shadrack.

Shadrack: Hi!

Daniel: Meshack.

Meshack: Hello, King!

Daniel: And Abednego.

Abednego: Right on!

Nebuchadnezzar: Boys, now that you are in Babylon, I'm gonna treat you right. You'll get royal treatment. You'll wear fine clothes. You'll eat what I eat. What do you think of that? Just come with me. *(They all leave. After a pause, Daniel and his three friends reappear)*

Daniel: This is terrible! We can't eat that food dedicated to idols! We can't drink that wine!

Shadrack: What can we do about it?

Meshack: He's the King!

Abednego: Everybody has to do what the King says.

Daniel: I think I have the answer. Steward! *(Steward appears)*

Steward: Well? What's wrong?

Daniel: Nothing, Steward. You are very kind. You do want us to please the King, don't you?

Steward: It's worth my life!

Daniel: Then we must eat the kind of food we eat at home or we'll be sick and puny.

Steward: Oh, no, you don't! The King says eat his food.

Daniel: Try us for ten days and see how we look.

Steward: The King will be angry!

Daniel: He'd be a lot angrier with four sick, skinny boys! *(All leave. Nebuchadnezzar returns)*

Nebuchadnezzar: Of course, I knew nothing about this. Nobody tells me anything! For three years I almost forgot those Hebrew boys. Well, don't you think a king has anything to do? There was the time the King of Tyre came to see me. A boring fellow! Did nothing but talk about himself! I couldn't get a word in edgewise! Then there was that delegation from Libya. All they wanted to do was eat and drink and watch dancing girls! Well, I couldn't hold up to it! Steward! *(Steward enters)*

Steward: Yes, your Majesty?

Nebuchadnezzar: *(Groaning)* My stomach feels awful! I can't face another rich meal!

Steward: Perhaps what the Hebrew boys eat would suit your Majesty better?

Nebuchadnezzar: What do you mean—what the Hebrew boys eat? Don't they eat what everyone else does?

Steward: Let me show you, your Majesty. *(He disappears, then reappears with the four boys)*

Steward: See how well they look, Sire?

Nebuchadnezzar: *(Surprised)* Yes, yes. What do they eat?

Daniel: Only the simplest foods—vegetables, whole grains and water, your Majesty. Just like at home. Our God wants

54

us to care for our bodies.

Nebuchadnezzar: Our God? Then he is responsible for your good appearance?

Daniel: Oh, yes.

Nebuchadnezzar: Then, we will all eat the simple food and we will give honor to your God! You may go while I think. *(All leave except Nebuchadnezzar)*

Nebuchadnezzar: I thought and thought. It was nice to know how good I had been to the Hebrew boys—well, my steward. But everything belongs to the King! Then it came to me! To celebrate I'd make an image! Everyone should worship my image! Quick, I'd issue an edict! *(He leaves and after a brief pause, the captain enters)*

Captain: Your Majesty! Your Majesty! Your Majesty! *(Nebuchadnezzar enters)*

Nebuchadnezzar: Quit shouting! What's the matter?

Captain: It's the Hebrew boys! Shadrack, Meshack and Abednego won't worship your image!

Nebuchadnezzar: Slaves can't defy the King! I knew it was a mistake trusting them! All the other slaves will be revolting! Not that some of them aren't revolting already. Captain, heat the furnace until it is seven times hotter than ever before! If they won't bow down—throw them into that fiery furnace!

Captain: Yes, your Majesty! *(He leaves)*

Nebuchadnezzar: Well, too bad. They were good boys. Handsome, too. Well, a king has to be obeyed. *(Captain reenters, agitated)*

Captain: Your Majesty! Your Majesty!

Nebuchadnezzar: Now what's the matter?

Captain: It's the Hebrew boys!

Nebuchadnezzar: Cooked to a cinder by now, I suppose.

Captain: No your Majesty! Oh, you won't believe it!

Nebuchadnezzar: Try me.

Captain: But you won't believe it! Those Hebrew boys are sitting in that furnace laughing and talking!

Nebuchadnezzar: I don't believe it!

Captain: I said you wouldn't believe it! But it's true! And that's not all!

Nebuchadnezzar: There's more?

Captain: Your Majesty, there's a fourth person in there —and I only put in three!

Nebuchadnezzar: Are you telling the truth? Then open that furnace and bring them to me at once! *(Captain leaves. A pause. He returns with the three boys and Daniel)*

Nebuchadnezzar: What are you doing here, Daniel? Were you the fourth person in that furnace?

Daniel: No, no, your Majesty! Not I. The fourth person was our God! He promised to be with my friends and he was!

Nebuchadnezzar: *(To boys and Captain)* Is this true? It wasn't Daniel in there?

All: No, your Majesty!

Nebuchadnezzar: Then—if your God can do this—he is the most powerful God of all! Captain, send out the messengers! Tell the people to worship the God of the Hebrews! Go at once! *(Captain leaves)* Now, Daniel, I have made a lot of mistakes in dealing with you and your friends. However, I am a progressive king. Tell me what I should learn from all this?

Daniel: Our God says we must not worship idols.

Nebuchadnezzar: Like mine?

Daniel: Yes, like yours. We must worship the one true God.

Nebuchadnezzar: Oh, I will! I promise!

Shadrack: Our God doesn't want us to defile our minds.

Meshack: Or our bodies.

Abednego: Our God just loves squares like us!

Shadrack: Hurray!

Meshack: Hurray!

Daniel: In return, our God promises to be with us wherever we are.

Nebuchadnezzar: Even in a—furnace?

Daniel: Even in a furnace! *(All leave)*

A Pretty Good Shot*

by Tom deGraaf

Willie, Cool Charlie

Willie: *(Enters with Cool Charlie, who has a rock in his hand)* Hey Cool Charlie . . . Where'd you get that rock?

Charlie: Wait a minute! Are you makin' *fun* of this sedimentary formation of granite crystal stalaganites?!?

Willie: No. I just was wonderin' about that dumb rock you got.

Charlie: Remind me to pulverize your shinbone later. . .

Willie: *(Pulls out small note pad—Makes note on it)* Let's see, remind Cool Charlie to pulverize my shinbone . . . What's that mean?

Charlie: *(Amazed)* Boy when they passed out brains you must have thought they said rain and told them you'd rather it didn't!

Willie: So what's with the dirt clod?

Charlie: This ain't no dirt clod, pumice face. This is the special rock that David used to slew Goliath!

Willie: *(Quizzical look)* . . . Slew who?

Charlie: *(Getting irritated)* Don't you know anything? I'm talkin' about David and Goliath. The guys who had one of the shortest fights in history.

Willie: Is it in the *Guinness Book of World Records*?

Charlie: I don't know . . . But it is in the Bible!

Willie: I don't ever remember hearing that story . . . would you mind telling it to me?

Charlie: *(Flattered)* Why certainly I'll tell it to you. I am known as one of the world's best storytellers!

Willie: Who's the other one? . . . Big Bird??

Charlie: Remind me to cauterize your kneecap . . .

Willie: *(Makes another note of it)*

Charlie: OK. Now here's the story, which I like to call "A Pretty Good Shot" . . . *(Proudly)* . . . not a bad title, huh?

Willie: *(Head tilting backwards—snores)*

Charlie: *(Judo-chops Willie's neck—thwack!)* Now pay attention lava lip! *(Resumes)* This Bible story is found in 1 Samuel 17:1-51. One day the children of Israel and the nasty persons of the Philistine army were having a war. Back in those days, they usually started by thinking up names to call each other. Well the Philistines were pretty good at that and in no time at all they were calling the children of Israel all kinds of things. Well, the children of Israel were God's people and so they were refraining from yelling back at the bad Philistine persons.

Well, after a while, this large giant-type soldier named Goliath got into the act and told the children of Israel that he was the strongest Philistine in the land and that he could punch out the whole army of Israel.

Willie: Sounds like a guy in my P.E. class at school. . .

Charlie: *(Glares)* As I was *saying*!, Goliath was the strongest guy in the Philistine army.

Willie: This guy in my P.E. class is pretty strong too . . . He doesn't use deodorant! *(Loves his own joke)* Ha Ha Ha ha!

Charlie: *(Judo-chops Willie. Falls down behind stage)* As I was saying. *(Clears throat)* As I was saying! *(Looks down where Willie has fallen)* . . . get up here marble head! *(Willie staggers up)* As I was saying, Goliath came out and started calling the children of Israel bad names. Well about this time, the king of Israel, Saul, was getting fed up with this giant Goliath, and began to look for someone in the army of Israel who would go out and fight him. The problem was that everybody in the children of Israel army knew Goliath, and they also knew he could beat 'em up with one finger stuck in his ear.

Well, it just so happened that David, a typical shepherd-type person, was just pulling into the army camp on his new sheep dog. David had come to bring his brothers, who were in the army, some kosher pickles and knew nothing about the giant Goliath and the terrible Philistines. Now David was quite a guy, even though he was just a kid. He heard Goliath bad-mouthing the children of Israel and went to King Saul and asked him why the giant was getting away with making fun of God and his children. David told King Saul that he was very put out with Goliath's attitude toward God and would it be OK if he went down and taught the giant a lesson?

King Saul told David that he shouldn't fight the giant but that if he wanted to, it was OK. So King Saul prayed for David and when David saw Goliath, David prayed for David. Finally God told David to go down to the river and get five rocks to throw at Goliath. Saul wondered how David was going to kill a giant with rocks, since Goliath regularly ate rocks with his morning cereal. Undaunted, David gathered his stones and went out to do battle with Goliath.

Willie: David should have called S. W. A. T.

Charlie: Quiet pebble-eyes! As I was saying—David went out to do battle with Goliath. When David got up close to Goliath he noticed that he was about *six* feet shorter than the giant.

Now Goliath got really mad. "Why'd they send out a *midget* to fight me?" he bellowed. David politely told him that he, in fact, was not a midget but was a smaller-type shepherd riding a very short sheep dog.

Well, to make a long story pretty much the same length, Goliath called David, the children of Israel, and God another bad name. David grabbed his slingshot and fired off a round of rocks that caught Goliath right between the eyes. The giant fell to the ground. David rushed over and cut off the giant's head just to make sure he wouldn't have any ideas about getting up again!

That made David a great hero. He had fought and beaten the giant, and now the whole nasty Philistine army split. God had saved David and the children of Israel!

Willie: Hey! That was a great story Cool Charlie!

Charlie: Why thank you cement brain.

Willie: (*Scratches his head*) Did you say that Goliath called David and God names? (*Takes rock from Cool Charlie—Starts eyeing Charlie with it*)

Charlie: Right . . . (*Notices rock*) . . . wonderful person!!

---

*Reprinted from *California Puppets*, Mill Valley, California. © Copyright, 1975. Used by permission.

57

Section III
SEASONAL

Love Stuff

by Sarah Walton Miller

Two Puppets

She: *(Gaily)* Oh, there you are. Isn't this fun?

He: *(Glumly)* No!

She: I can hardly wait for what's coming next. It's _____ *(insert next activity)*. You'll enjoy that!

He: *(Groaning)* No, no, no!

She: *(Surprised)* Why not?

He: *(Disgustedly)* All this love stuff!

She: *(Ecstatically)* I love the love stuff.

He: *(Making a sound of disgust)* Yech!

She: *(Sighs loudly)* So romantic! So—so—

He: Sickening!

She: *(Coyly)* Oh, now, you don't mean that! You know what's the matter? You just want to get in on it yourself! *(Moves over and snuggles against him)* Here I am! Snuggling right up to you. *(Drops voice into a low sexy tone)* Look into my eyes! What do you see?

He: *(Moving away and looking)* Bloodshot. Your eyes are bloodshot.

She: *(Annoyed)* Not that! Look again. Can't you see the lovelight shining there? . . . Now how do you feel?

He: *(Backing away)* N-nervous!

She: *(Playfully)* Oh, you are such a tease. How would you like to kiss me? *(Lifts face)*

He: Not much!

She: Are you playing hard to get? Oh, no, no! I know what it is—you are just trying to act like a *gentleman*.

He: *(In relief)* Yeah! Yeah! That's it! I'm a gentleman! That's me—a real gentleman.

She: *(Tenderly)* Well. Baby, you needn't try to conceal your true feelings from me. I'm very open-minded. Any time you want to kiss me—just say the magic word!

He: *(Frantically)* I don't know the word!

She: I'll tell you. The word is—

He: No! Don't tell me! I don't want to know the word! Yech!

She: *(Grabbing him)* Baby! That's the word! *(She pulls him out of view)*

Miss Mary's Toy Shop

by Joan King

Miss Mary: Shop Owner *(person in front of curtain)*
Annie: Rag Doll *(person in front of curtain)*
Jack: Jack-in-the-box *(dresses as clown in a decorated TV box in front of curtain)*

Puppets: Betsy *(cow)*, Lisa *(toy)*, Henry *(toy-giraffe)*, First Whatzit, Second Whatzit, Poof *(a friendly ghost)*, Christmas Lion, Two Visitors, Alfred *(toy)*, Robin *(toy)*, Owlfie *(toy)*

Props: Jack's box, Christmas tree, Jack-O-Lantern, Saxophone, Pedal Car, Horn, Jack's Book

(Four toys are asleep on the curtain, Annie is seated on stool asleep. Lights are dim. Music, "Carol of the Bells," begins. Miss Mary enters, wakes Annie. Annie wakes toys. Music fades)

Jack: Hi! My name is Jack. I live in Miss Mary's Toy Shop. That was Miss Mary and Annie waking the toys. I have a book down here somewhere that tells how Annie became Miss Mary's special helper . . . where is that book *(Fumbles in box)* . . . Here it is. *(Opens book)* This is the story of Annie's Very Special Christmas . . . Once upon a time in a little toy shop there was a very shy doll named Annie. She loved the toy shop and Miss Mary. Annie was afraid when Christmas came she would be sold to a little girl and have to leave the toy shop. But one day Miss Mary made a very special announcement.

Mary: Good morning, everyone.

All: Good morning, Miss Mary.

Mary: Is everyone ready to open the shop and see all the boys and girls?

Betsy: Miss Mary, may I stay here and live with you? I like the toy shop.

Mary: I'd like to keep all of you, but it's Christmas, and little boys and girls want you to come live with them. But . . . . I've been thinking. The true Christmas spirit is missing in the toy shop, and I'll let the toy who can find it, stay here forever.

Lisa: You mean forever and ever?

Mary: Yes. The toy who finds the true meaning of Christmas and brings Christmas spirit to the toy shop can be my helper and live here forever.

Betsy: Did you hear that everybody? What we need around here is a little Christmas.

(Puppets sing "We Need A Little Christmas")

Jack: And that's how the day began. In the book that's Chapter 1. Now, why don't we see what happened in Chapter 2? *(Fumbles)* Oh, I've lost the book again. Here it is *(Reads)* Chapter 2. All the animals got to work and started making plans to show Miss Mary the true meaning of Christmas. Henry G. Raff was the first toy with an idea.

Henry: Miss Mary.

Mary: Yes, Henry.

Henry: I have written, directed, and produced a play about Christmas spirit. And, of course, I am the star . . . Would you like to see it?

Mary: Yes, Henry. Go on with your play.

Henry: Ladies and gentlemen. The play you are about to see is written, directed, and produced by Mr. Henry G. Raff, a rising young musical star. The setting is a small town named Christmastown where the Christmas spirit is kept alive by people who sing Christmas carols all year around. Lights, please. *(Christmas tree up)*

First Visitor: What a pretty tree!

Second Visitor: Doesn't this town have the Christmas spirit?

Henry: Hello there. Are you strangers in Christmastown? I'm the mayor of Christmastown, Mayor Raff.

First Visitor: Yes. We heard about your Christmas spirit and came for a visit.

Second Visitor: How do you keep it all year round?

Henry: By singing Christmas carols. As mayor, I'd like to invite you to sing a carol with me so that you too can feel like a part of the Christmas spirit.

Visitors: Oh, thank you. We love to sing Christmas carols.
(Puppets sing ''Sleigh Bells'')
First Visitor: We really enjoyed that, Mayor Raff. May we see the rest of your town, now that we've got the Christmas Spirit?
Henry: Of course. Right this way. *(They exit. Whatzits enter)*
First Whatzit: Hee! Hee! Look at the Christmas tree.
Second Whatzit: Before long it'll be gone along with all the Christmas spirit in this town.
First Whatzit: Poof! Where's that spook? He's always getting lost. Poof! *(Poof backs up and bumps into them)*
Second Whatzit: Poof, where've you been?
Poof: Oh, just looking the town over. Really is a lot of Christmas spirit around here. Everybody's singing carols and having fun.
Second Whatzit: Fun? Have you already forgotten why we came to town? We came to destroy the Christmas spirit by turning Christmastown into Halloweentown.
First Whatzit: And you're the one with all the poofing talent. You're supposed to poof all the Christmas spirit away so everybody will sing Halloween songs instead of Christmas songs.
Poof: Where do I start?
First Whatzit: With the Christmas tree.
Poof: OK. Poof. Poof. Poof *(Lights flash, Jack-O-Lantern replaces tree)* How's that? Not every spook can make such a big Jack-O-Lantern from a Christmas tree. Only Poof the Spook—that's me.
First Whatzit: Yeah. You're loaded with talent, Poof.
Second Whatzit: How about poofing up some Halloween carolers for us?
Poof: OK. Poof. Poof. Poof. *(They exit)*
(Henry, and two carolers enter singing Halloween carols)
Henry: What's heppened to us? Why are we singing Halloween songs? Where's our Christmas spirit?
Caroler: I think somebody's been up to something.
First Whatzit: *(Enters)* Hee, hee. We certainly have. How do you like the spell we've cast over Christmastown?
Henry: I don't like it and we're going to do something about it.
First Whatzit: There's nothing you can do. We've turned Christmastown into Halloweentown forever. You'll never be able to sing Christmas carols again. *(Exits)*
Caroler: What are we going to do?
Henry: Well, I can just think of one way to do away with

the Whatzits. And, that's to find the Christmas Lion.
Caroler: But, I haven't seen him in a long time. Where could he be?
Henry: I don't know, but as mayor I'm going to send a search party all over Christmastown. Whatzits are allergic to lion dust. With one swish of his tail, the Christmas Lion will make them start sneezing so hard they'll leave Christmastown forever.
Caroler: Well, let's find the Lion without wasting anymore time.
(They exit, Lion enters, Henry re-enters)
Henry: There he is. There's the Christmas Lion. Mr. Lion, I've looked everywhere for you. Have you heard what the Whatzits and Poof the Spook have done to Christmastown? Can you help us? *(Lion nods yes)* Then wait by the Jack-O-Lantern. The Whatzits will be along soon. Just shake your tail and dust them all over with lion dust so they'll leave.
(Lion nods yes. Whatzits enter)
First Whatzit: We've done a great job. It's now Halloweentown.
Second Whatzit: Oh no, Look! The Christmas Lion!
First Whatzit: No, no. Ah-chooo.
Second Whatzit: Look, he's shaking lion dust on us. Ah-chooo.
First Whatzit: Ah-choo. Please stop. We'll get Poof to change everything back. We'll leave Christmastown forever. Ah-choo.
Second Whatzit: Just don't scatter any more Lion Dust on us. Ah-choo.
First Whatzit: Poof. Hurry, change everything back. Ah-choo.
(They exit, Poof enters)
Poof: I'll tell you what. Being a spook for those Whatzits sure is tiring. ''Change this, Poof. Change that, Poof.'' That's all I ever hear. Well . . . Here goes again. Poof. Poof. Poof. *(Lights flash and he exits)*
Henry: Hurrah for you Christmas Lion! You saved the Christmas spirit. Now we can all sing a Christmas carol to celebrate. Benny has his saxophone. Let's sing ''Jingle Bell Rock.'' *(They sing and Benny plays)*
Mary: Henry, that was very interesting. I'm sure you're going to be one of the best producers, directors, and writers. Christmas wouldn't seem right without Christmas carols, but there's something else about Christmas that makes it more special than just a time to sing.
Henry: That's perfectly all right, my dear. We shall simply try harder next time. *(Exits as Annie enters)*
Mary: Why, Annie, what's wrong?

Annie: Miss Mary, all of the other toys are so busy planning their plays and I can't think of a thing. I think I know what Christmas is about, but I'm not as smart as Henry. I could never produce and direct a play.

Mary: Oh, Annie, don't worry about the toys and what they're doing. You tell about the true Christmas spirit in your own way. Sometimes the simplest way is best.

Annie: Maybe if I look for ideas in some books, I can find what the true meaning of Christmas is.

Mary: Of course, Annie, Let's look for some books.

(They exit, Jack enters)

Jack: Well, that's how Chapter 2 ends. Annie started looking for a book about the true meaning of Christmas, and Henry started producing, directing, and writing another play. Meanwhile, in Chapter 3, Alfred the Inchworm began a campaign to encourage the sale of pedal car licenses. *(Fumbles)* Chapter 3, let's see, math is one of my best subjects . . . before four. *(Reads)* Alfred the Inchworm was the next toy to present an idea to Miss Mary. Alfred had recently been elected deputy sheriff, and he was really taking his new job seriously. It seems he came across his idea for the true meaning of Christmas while patrolling pedal cars. *(Alfred enters)*

Alfred: Oh, hello there. If you don't know me, please allow me to introduce myself. Name's Alfred. Deputy Alfred since the last election. Now . . . ah, I say, whose pedal car is that? Miss Mary, Miss Mary. *(She enters)*

Mary: You called Alfred?

Alfred: Listen, as deputy in charge of pedal cars, I need to check out the owner of that car over there.

Mary: I believe that pedal car belongs to Robin.

Alfred: I'll put an all-points bulletin out on Robin.

Mary: Wait a minute, Alfred. Is that necessary?

Alfred: As a public servant I must fulfill my obligation. We officers of the law must protect the American public from all criminals.

Mary: But Robin's not a criminal!

Alfred: Where duty calls, I must answer! *(They exit. Robin enters)*

Robin: Rrrrr. Hey, out of the way. I'm in a hurry.

Toy: What's the rush, Robin?

Robin: To see how fast my new pedal car will go.

Toy: I haven't seen one like that. Where'd you get it?

Robin: My grandmother gave it to me for Christmas. What did your grandmother give you?

Toy: A horn. It's nice and shiny, and honks really loud.

Robin: I wish I had a horn for my pedal car. *(Alfred enters)*

Alfred: Pedal car? Did someone say, pedal car?

Toy: Yes, Officer Alfred. Robin's grandmother gave her a new pedal car for Christmas.

Alfred: I hope she gave you a pedal car license, too.

Robin: Pedal car license?

Alfred: Yes. Pedal car license. As deputy in charge of patrolling pedal cars, tricycles, and all other nonmotor vehi-cles with three wheels or more, I am required by law to check all owners of above mentioned vehicles for licenses.

Robin: But, Grandmother didn't give me one.

Alfred: Just like the older generation. Irresponsible.

Toy: How can Robin get a license, Officer Alfred?

Alfred: How old are you, Kid?

Robin: Three years old.

Alfred: That settles that. Can't get a pedal car license till you're four. Too bad Grandma didn't give you a tricycle. You can get that license when you're three.

Robin: *(Crying)* I wanta ride my pedal car now. . .

Alfred: Hold it kid. *(Cries louder)* Now kid, I'm sorry. You'll have to find an older person to drive that car. *(Exits)*

Toy: Wait a minute, Robin. I've got an idea. I'm four years old and it's Christmas and Christmas is a time for presents, right?

Robin: Right, and I can't ride my present. *(Cries)*

Toy: Yes you can, listen. We haven't exchanged gifts yet. If I give you half my horn, and you give me half your car, I can drive, cause I'm old enough, and you can blow the horn if we put it on the car.

Robin: Yes, then we'd both have a pedal car with a horn!

Toy: Right. Let's go get my horn.

Robin: And a pedal car license for you. *(Horn attached to car)*

(Robin toots horn as Alfred enters)

Alfred: Well, looks like Robin's in her car after all!

Toy: Because I'm four and I have a license, Officer Alfred.

Alfred: Well, I'm happy. Now the streets are safe again.

Robin: And we're happy because we exchanged gifts. I'm so glad Christmas is a time for giving. *(They exit. Jack enters)*

Jack: Miss Mary agreed with Alfred and the others that giving is an important part of Christmas, but still something was missing. That brings us to the fourth and last chapter. Annie was searching for a book, remember? Well, she has my sympathy because I can't find mine. Anyway, this is what happens in Chapter 4.

Mary: *(Enters. Hangs a star on the tree)* There, that looks nice. *(Annie enters)*

Annie: Miss Mary? I've found a book which tells the true meaning of Christmas. It's called the Bible.

Mary: Good Annie. You've found just what I've been wanting to hear. Tell us about the first Christmas.

Annie: This is the Christmas story *(Reads Luke 2:1-20. Then she sings "He shall Live Again" from the musical Good News)* This is what Christmas is . . . a day of celebration . . . a celebration in honor of our Lord's birthday.

Mary: Thank you for showing us the real meaning of Christmas. You deserve being Miss Mary's special helper. Now we can wish everybody a Merry Christmas in the true Christmas spirit. *(All sing "We Wish You a Merry Christmas")*

The Lottie Moon Story*

by Tom deGraaf

Sally, Willie, Dad

Dad: *(Enters tired, has newspaper and begins to read)* My feet are killing me! Corn City. Wouldn't you know it! The *(team)* got beat again . . . *(Reads on)* . . . Hey, that sure sounds like a great fishing boat . . . I wonder how much they want for it . . . Well, it sounds like the economy is about to get back on its feet again . . . *(Perks up)* Would you look at that! *(Church member)* got arrested last night for impersonating Santa Claus without a license! ''*(Church member)* was arrested on mainstreet last night by local police for illegally staging a Christmas parade. *(Member)* was cited for trying to pass off several cows and a rental trailer as a sleigh with eight tiny reindeer.''

Willie and Sally: *(Come rushing in, scare Dad and paper goes flying)*

Sally: Dad, me and Willie are bored stiff.

Willie: Yeah, here it is the second day of Christmas vacation and we can't think of one thing to do . . .

Dad: *(Regains composure)* . . . You do pretty well as a riot simulator . . .

Sally: *(Gets idea)* Dad! Tell us a story! Tell us a story!

Willie: Yeah! Tell us a story! Tell us a Christmas story! Will ya? Huh? Will ya, Dad?

Dad: Will you promise to be quiet and listen?

Sally: Yes! We'll be quiet! *(To Willie)* Won't we!?

Willie: *(Excited, yells)* yeaaaa!! Dad's gonna tell us a Christmas story! *(Yells again)* YeeeeYahooooo!! Yeeeeouch!

Dad: *(Rubbing ears)* Quiet, remember, son? Quiet!

Willie: Sorry. But you're on my foot. *(Looks down)*

Dad: *(Looks down)* Oh excuse me. Now which story would you like to hear: *The Grinch Who Stole Christmas? The Chipmunk Who Ate Santa's C.B. Radio?*

Willie: Aw, that's kid's stuff. We want to hear something neat.

Sally: Yeah—Something really neat that'll help get us into the Christmas spirit.

Dad: Well, how would you like to hear the true story of the most famous Christmas missionary lady in the whole world?

Sally: Yeah! That's more like it!

Willie: *(Jumps up and down)* Yeaaa! That sounds like a really interesting story, Dad. Tell it right now, OK?

Dad: OK. But Willie you move over a little!

Willie: How come?

Dad: You jumped on my foot. Smashed three corns.

Willie: *(Moves back)* . . . Sorry.

Dad: OK. Here is the story about the most famous Christmas missionary lady in the world—Charlotte Moon. Or better known as Lottie Moon. Are you kids comfy?

Willie and Sally: Yep. Go ahead. We're listening to every word.

Dad: Well, Lottie Moon was born at Christmas time, way back in the year 1840. She lived in Virginia, near the homes of Presidents Thomas Jefferson and James Monroe. I'll bet you didn't know that, did you?

Sally: Nope.

Dad: When Lottie got older, she began teaching school in a little town named Cartersville, down in Georgia. Lottie loved children. She even taught Sunday School down at First Baptist there in Cartersville. In fact, Lottie loved teaching about God so much that in Feb., 1873, she dedicated her life to be a missionary to China. It sure wasn't an easy thing to do, but Lottie packed up her belongings, said good-bye to her family and friends, and left for China in 1878.

Willie: Now! I've heard of going off to summer camp, but going off to China? Did she get homesick?

Sally: Was the food bad?

Dad: That's not the half of it! When Lottie arrived in China she found a strange and often dangerous land. The people did not trust her because she was a stranger to them. It took Lottie quite a while to even learn the language so she could make friends.

Sally: I'll bet her first Christmas there was awful . . . No friends, no Christmas tree, no presents . . .

Dad: Eventually Lottie did have friends, the children!

Willie: Children?

Dad: That's right. Lottie started a small Bible school in her village and many of the children became good friends with her. And you know what else? The children brought their mothers to meet Lottie.

Sally: That was sweet.

Dad: It sure was. But the more people Lottie met, the more she noticed most of them never had enough to eat. Lottie felt sorry for them and gave her own food away so often she didn't have enough to eat either.

Willie: How awful!

Dad: Well, it was, Willie. But you know the thing that upset Lottie the most was that many of her Chinese friends had never heard about Jesus. And even though she tried to tell them, only the women and children would listen to her. None of the Chinese men would come to hear her talk about the Bible or God.

Sally: Boy! That must have been discouraging.

Dad: It was. As a matter of fact, from the time Lottie gave her life as a missionary to China in 1878 to the time when the Chinese men finally asked her to explain the gospel, thirteen years had gone by.

Sally: Maybe those men back then were just poor conversationalists.

Dad: Well, you have to remember that to them, Lottie Moon was a stranger from another land, with a religion that was totally different from their own. But once they finally learned to trust Lottie, the people kept on coming and coming, asking to know more about Jesus. You know what they began to call Lottie?

Willie: What?

Dad: "The Heavenly Book Visitor."

Sally: That's so cute! She must have really loved that after the time spent trying to make friends!

Dad: She did. In fact, Lottie loved the Chinese people so much, she only returned to the United States once in the twenty-four years she lived in China.

Willie: She only came home one time in twenty-four years? She must have really gotten homesick.

Dad: She did. But Lottie had loved ones in China too who needed to hear and learn about Jesus. Lottie's love and concern became so great for the Chinese people that she began writing letters to the Southern Baptists in the United States, urging them to organize their Missionary Program. Lottie felt that through an organized campaign, more Christians in the United States could be shown the tremendous need for missionaries in other countries. She hoped that more people would give their money to help pay the cost of spreading the gospel in lands such as China. And do you know what happened?

Sally: I know—we have the Lottie Moon Christmas Offering now.

Dad: Right! Ladies in Missionary Unions all over the Convention began to spring into action for Lottie Moon and all the other missionaries who were struggling to tell the story of Jesus. Soon, reinforcements began to arrive in China and in other lands. Well, Lottie Moon had accomplished two goals by the time she died in 1912. She had been a good and faithful missionary to the Chinese people, and had sparked a new and sustained commitment in the heart of Southern Baptists for foreign missions. And that's how the Lottie Moon Christmas Offering came into being.

Sally: That was a beautiful story Dad.

Willie: Where does the Lottie Moon Offering go?

Dad: Well, Lottie herself said that since the greatest gift ever given was given at Christmas—Jesus—that Christmas is the best time for Christians to give that same gift to people in other lands. In other words, when we give money at Christmas, we are each helping to send a missionary to tell someone about Jesus.

Sally: *(Hugs Dad)* I really feel great about Christmas now. As a matter of fact, I'm going to give some money next Sunday to Lottie Moon's missionaries.

Willie: *(Hugs Dad too. All three are hugging)* I'm going to give some money too.

Sally: *(Still hugging)* You don't have any money.

Willie: *(Sheepishly)* Oh yeah . . . Can you lend me some?

Dad: That's really great that you kids want to do something for the missionaries . . . Now could you do something for me? *(They all are still hugging, Dad points down)*

Willie: HeeHee. *(Backs off)* Sorry about your toe Dad.

Sally: *(Backs off)* Yeah. Me too. Sorry . . .

Dad: *(Trying to conceal pain)* That's quite all right . . . What say we all go into the kitchen and find the Epsom salt. I want to soak my feet while I still have 'em left . . .

Willie: Right Dad. Will you tell us another story?

Sally: We wanta hear another Christmas story Dad!

Willie: *(Jumps up and down—chants)* We want a story. We want a story! *(Lands on Dad's toe again! Looks down)*

Dad: *(Looks down—then slowly at audience)* . . . I don't know if my bunions can take another story!

Christmas Is a Live Turkey

by Carl Marder

Betsy (little girl), Dumpsie (dog), Mother, Father

Betsy: *(Enters singing a made-up song with Dumpsie following her)* It's Christmas time, it's Christmas time,
It's Christmas time, hurrah!
It's Christmas time, it's Christmas time,
It's Christmas time, hurray!
Oh, Dumpsie, you don't know what I'm singing about, do you? This is your very first Christmas. You'll love it. It's the most beautimous time in the whole year. *(She exits singing)*

Dumpsie: This Christmas must really be something special. I've never seen Betsy or anyone so excited. I can hardly wait to see it . . . if it's something you see . . . or maybe it's something to eat. I'd like that. That's probably what it is . . . something to eat! Yum, yum!

(Mother, Father enter. Father carries tree)

Mother: I know it's almost Christmas. Why do you think I'm so worried? Put the Christmas tree in the corner.

Dumpsie: It's a tree? Christmas is a tree? Dog-nab it! Even a decorated tree can't make me happy.

Mother: *(Whispers)* Now help me get the turkey and the gifts out of the car and bring them in while Betsy's out of the room. *(They exit)*

Dumpsie: It's a turkey! That's more like it. Christmas is a turkey . . . and it's gifts. That's good too. *(Pause)* She said she was worried. I wonder why Christmas would make her worried. I wouldn't worry about gifts and a turkey! Oh, oh. Maybe the turkey is alive! That's it, Christmas is a live turkey.

(Father, Mother enter)

Father: *(Tired, angry)* The gifts are in the closet, the turkey's in the freezer. We've got the tree and it's deco-rated. Now what? Christmas gets to be more and more trouble every year. I'll be glad when it's over so I can spend my Saturdays on the golf course again.

Mother: Well, it's not over yet, so don't relax. Betsy's bicycle has to be put together and her Weepy Wetsy doll needs batteries.

Father: For Pete's sake! Why didn't we order the bike assembled?

Mother: Because of fifteen dollars!

Father: You could have gotten the batteries while we were out.

Mother: Don't start an argument. I'm as tired and disgusted with this whole Christmas mess as you are.

Father: Thank goodness it's only once a year. *(They exit)*

Dumpsie: Christmas evidently isn't a live turkey . . . they put it in the freezer. It's not even something to eat. It sounds like it's a lot of trouble. I wonder why Betsy was so happy? Maybe it's only good for kids and dogs.

Betsy: *(Sings as she crosses stage)*
It's Christmas time, it's Christmas time,
It's Christmas time, sing hi!
It's Christmas time, it's Christmas time,
It's Christmas time, sing low!
If I don't get a stove that cooks real food,
I'll die, die, die.

Mother: *(Enters brings table with a manger scene. Jesus is in the manger)* Out of the way, Dumpsie. You're right where we always put the manger scene. *(Dumpsie moves)* Now, that finally finishes the decorating. *(Exits)*

Dumpsie: *(Looks at manger scene)* A baby . . . lying in the hay? I wonder what this has to do with Christmas?

The First Christmas Night

by Sarah Walton Miller

Animal One, Animal Two

One: Push me right out of my warm bed, will he? What's he up to now? A sheep ought to have some rights!
(Two appears)
Two: What are you doing over here?
One: Watching to see what he's up to. He's never driven us out of our warm beds before.
Two: I know what he's up to. I could hear his wife outside. He's giving your bed to people.
One: *(Shocked)* Oh, no! People in a stable? With all the rooms he has in that inn? Of course I knew he was stingy. Have you noticed the quality of the feed he's been doling out lately? But to take a sheep's bed for people—well, that's a bit much!
Two: Where's your little Lambie Pie? I don't see him?
One: Mrs. Cow let him bed down with her calf.
Two: Mrs. Cow? I don't believe it! She's never been friendly.
One: He went over there and she didn't push him away. I let him stay because it's warm there.
Two: Listen!
One: What is it?
Two: People coming. Here, look! You can see. *(They move a little and look at supposed interior of stable)*
Two: Look! There's a woman. *(Sympathetically)* Why the poor thing's sick!
One: *(Impatiently)* No, silly, she's not sick! Not sick sick anyway. She's about to have a baby.
Two: Oh. Out here? In the stable? What can that landlord be thinking of?
One: Well, it didn't hurt me any. Or Lambie Pie either.
Two: Oh, you're a sheep. People aren't as well-built.

One: *(Proudly)* That's true, isn't it? Well, since this is the best bed we'll have tonight, why don't we try to get some sleep? Goodnight.
Two: Goodnight.
(They lean against each other and snore gently for about six snores. Then Two wakes up. Moves and looks back into stable. Comes and shakes One excitedly)
Two: Wake Up! Wake up!
One: *(Yawning)* What's the hurry? We're not going anywhere.
Two: Come look!
(They move over and look toward stable; then return)
One: *(Pleased)* Well, what do you know! A baby!
Two: *(Proudly)* Right here in our stable!
One: Did you see? Its bed is right in Mrs. Cow's feeding trough! She'll be livid. You know how persnickety she is.
Two: Those people couldn't know that. *(Sentimentally)* They looked so proud, didn't they?
One: I know that feeling. Why, when my Lambie Pie was born, I knew right off that there was a lamb to be proud of!
Two: Wonder what it is?
One: A baby, of course. A people baby.
Two: *(Impatiently)* I mean—a boy or girl?
One: Well, if it's a girl—poor thing! The way the world is, females have a hard time.
Two: And if it's a boy?
One: Oh, a boy has a chance of making something of himself. He'll have it easy. You just mark my words! If that baby's a boy, he'll have it easy!
(They leave. At this point, with youth and adults, have discussion. There are many avenues open.)

The New Year's Resolution*

by Tom deGraaf

Willie, Sally, Weird Rodney, Dad, Pastor

Sally: *(Enters hurriedly, starts writing on paper, stops, starts again, stops in disgust)* Aw phooey! Here it is the middle of January already and I haven't even been able to come up with one decent New Year's resolution!
(In background a terrible violin begins to play, accompanied by howling dog) How can I even think straight around here let alone write any New Year's resolutions? Weird Rodney and that violin are enough to drive anybody crazy!

Willie: *(Enters)* In your case a short walk would likely be enough. What are you doing anyway Sally? *(Violin stops)*

Sally: I'm trying to make a list of New Year's resolutions. Dad said everybody ought to do it as an exercise in self-control and willpower.

Willie: I never make New Year's resolutions! You know why?

Sally: Why?

Willie: I asked you. I don't know, myself. . .

Dad: *(Enters)* Hi Willie. Hi Sally.

Willie and Sally: Hi Dad!

Dad: What are you kids up to?

Sally: *(Frustrated)* I'm trying to write some New Year's resolutions, but I can't think of any! I'm getting disgusted too. *(Violin, dog's howling starts)* Oooo that Weird Rodney next door is driving me crazy!

Dad: Try not to let it bother you too much Dear. I had a long talk with Rodney's mother about it and she said it's the only constructive thing she can get Rodney to do. So we'll just have to bear it. *(Violin stops, dog continues to howl. Voice yells at dog, "Shut up dummy, he's done playin'!" The dog chokes off his last beautiful howl)*

Willie: Brother! That dog's gotten so weird from Rodney's

playing that he's started chasing parked cars again.

Dad: You know what? I have an idea for a resolution!

Sally: *(Excited)* What is it Daddy? What is it?!

Dad: Why don't you resolve never to let Rodney's violin playing upset you. You might even begin to enjoy it!

Sally: It won't work. I tried that idea last year on the preacher's sermons. . .

Dad: Sally!!! That's a terrible thing to say! Besides, it's not in the script.

Sally: I know—I just couldn't resist it. *(To Pastor in audience)* You can take a joke, can't you Pastor? Can't you? Huh?

Pastor: *(From audience. Sounding unrehearsed)* Let's put it this way; how do you feel about becoming a unitarian?

Sally: *(To Dad)* Does that mean he can't take a joke?

Willie: I would say that's a pretty fair guess. Yeah. . .

Sally: Oh . . . *(Violin and dog start)* Oooooooo, my ears! *(Yells)* Weird Rodney, you and that dumb dog shut up right now!!!

Dad: Sally! How could you say such a thing?

Sally: Well . . . All that noise they're making is giving my earwax ripples. What am I supposed to do?

Dad: You probably went and hurt Weird, uh, Rodney's feelings.

Willie: I hope the dog at least didn't hear you yell like that . . . *(The dog cries—Ahooo)* Way to go.

Sally: You even hurt the dog's feelings.

Rodney: *(Enters shyly with violin)* Excuse me. Someone said I was playing too loudly?

Sally: Too loudly? It sounded like a concert for a violin and pet clinic!

Rodney: I'm sorry if my doggie was singing too loudly, but he can't help himself sometimes.

Sally: So why don't you play something he doesn't know?

Dad: We didn't mean to interrupt you Rodney. And Sally was only kidding about your violin playing and the dog.

Sally: I was? *(Dad glares)* Oh right . . . Yeah . . . I was just kidding Weird Rodney. I think you have a, uh, unique ability.

Rodney: *(Flattered)* Why thank you very much Miss Sally. I'd be happy to play for you any time.

Willie and Sally: *(Off-guardedly sour)* We know. *(Dad clears voice, looks at Willie and Sally. They change to excited attitude)* We mean . . .

Sally: We know you'd play for us anytime and we'd really love it! We'd love it won't we, Dad?

Dad: *(On the spot)* Uh, Sure! You can play for us anytime.

Rodney: *(Honored)* Oh thank you Mr. Weekers! In fact . . . *(Thinks)* . . . In fact, I'm making a New Year's resolution here and now for me and my doggie to play a song for you every day of the week this whole year!

Dad: Er, That's fine Rodney . . .

Willie: Yeah . . . Uh, thanks a lot. *(Sally cries)*

Dad: *(Reprimanding)* Uh, Sally!!

Sally: *(Crying, tries to cover up)* I'm crying for . . . joy, Dad, crying . . . for . . . ulp . . . joy . . . *(Holds head in hand)*

Rodney: *(Touched)* You're all so nice, and I just want to say a big thank you and not to worry. I won't fail you! I'll play for you every night over the fence! Bye Bye! *(Exits)* *(They stare at each other in shocked silence)*

Sally: *(Slowly picks up paper, wads and throws it away)* Nice going Dad. Every night for the next year my eardrums will play host to Weird Rodney and his singing dog. So

much for New Year's resolutions.

Willie: So much for peace and quiet.

Dad: Well, look at the bright side though. You've gained a friend.

Sally: *(Interrupts)* And a dog.

Willie: *(Interrupts)* And a year without sleep.

Dad: And a chance to practice a little willpower and self-control—something we all need. It'll be good for you! *(Violin and dog start up again. They stare at each other, holding ears, music stops)*

On second thought, why don't we make a New Year's resolution to invite Weird Rodney and his dog over for ice cream the minute we hear 'em start playing each night?

Sally: Right on Dad! Let's get 'em before they start again!

Willie: You said it! Let's go Sally! *(They exit)*

Dad: *(Starts to exit, stops)* You know folks, a resolution is a tricky thing. Sometimes it gets you into trouble, sometimes it keeps you out of trouble. But mostly a New Year's resolution is just an honest attempt by our subconscious mind to admit how bad we fouled up last year so we won't do it again this year! *(Violin, dog start up)* Well it sounds like I'd better invite Rodney and his dog over for some ice cream real quick. *(Starts to exit, stops)* Pastor, Sally didn't mean to joke about your sermon a while ago.

Pastor: I know!

Dad: But keep an eye on your deacons. Just in case you find an ice cream in the offering plate next Sunday. *(Exits)*

The Watchers

by Carl Marder

Two Puppets Dressed as Children

She: I love to come to the art gallery and see all the pretty pictures.

He: I'm going to be a painter some day.

She: Will you paint a picture of me?

He: Maybe, I don't know. *(They approach picture of Crucifixion)*

She: What's this picture?

He: It's Jesus on the Cross.

She: It looks like he's hanging there.

He: He is—or, he was.

(The following lines should be said slowly, allowing time between each line. Also, these are children's observations, not necessarily emotional)

She: What's that on his head?

He: A crown made out of thorns.

She: Pushed onto his head?

He: Yeah.

She: How is he hanging there?

He: They nailed his hands and feet to the cross with a great big hammer.

She: It must have taken long nails.

He: It did.

She: He must have bled a lot of blood.

He: He did.

She: Did it hurt?

He: More than anything I know about.

She: Did he cry?

He: Sure he cried. He was hurt. He suffered from a lot of pain, he died, and they buried him.

She: Where were all the good people?

He: Around

She: What were they doing?

He: Watching.

She: He let them put the thorn crown on his head? He let them put nails in his hands and feet? He let them watch him suffer and watch him cry?

He: Yes.

She: This picture makes me very sad.

He: Me too. But it's not the end. He arose from the dead.

She: He did?

He: So people could be saved.

She: Even the ones that watched?

He: Even the ones that watched; even the ones that watch.

She: Why?

He: Because he loves everybody in the whole world.

She: I wouldn't watch him be crucified.

He: I wouldn't either. I'd want to do something for Him.

She: Me, too. *(They exit)*

Father's Day

by Carroll Bryant Brown

Debbie, Bud

Bud: *(Enters whistling)* Man, what a beautiful day! Let's see—what can I do today? Ahm!! Throw rocks at the next train—naw. Maybe I'll sneak down to the park and hide bicycles—yeah! Ha! Then hide and watch people look for them. Ha! Ha! Ha! *(Debbie enters carrying a gift. Bud whistles at her and shouts)* Hi there, Debbie. Where are you going with that present? Somebody got a birthday party today? That would be fun. I'm in a mood for a good time. Let's go!

Debbie: Oh, hi, Bud. No, this is a gift for my dad. It's Father's Day, and I want to show how much I really love him.

Bud: Ah, he knows you love him. Why the gift and all that bit?

Debbie: Well, when you love someone, you like to do nice things for them. Today is Father's Day, and I'm doing something nice for Dad.

Bud: Yeah. Well, I'd get a present, but . . . well . . . I forgot all about it. I'll just tell Dad that I love him.

Debbie: Oh, Bud! You don't have to get a present. You could do something special for him.

Bud: I could?

Debbie: Sure!

Bud: What? Give him an IOU?

Debbie: No, you could help him with some of his tasks this week, or even make him something. That would mean more than just buying him a present.

Bud: Wow, that's an idea. Maybe I could mow the yard tomorrow and surprise him when he gets home. He'd probably faint from the shock!

Debbie: That would be wonderful!

Bud: Yeah, I guess it would be fun. Thanks, Debbie, for the idea. I feel happy inside just thinking about it. Dads are really pretty special. Hey, beautiful, maybe I'll walk you home. *(Debbie acts embarrassed and shy)*

Debbie: Oh, I'm not going home right now. I'm on my way to Sunday School.

Bud: Sunday School!!! Are you kidding? What are you going to do—make paper dolls?

Debbie: No!! Of course not! You know God is our real father. He gives us things we need everyday. He loves us so much that all our sins can be forgiven, if we love his Son. It makes us want to do kind things for others.

Bud: Gee, I never thought about it like that. I wonder how many people are celebrating the real Father's Day? But, I've been pretty bad. I guess God wouldn't want me to be one of his kids.

Debbie: Of course he does. He loves all of us the same. But it is only when we love him and his Son Jesus that we come to know him as a father. Then he is so happy!

Bud: Great! I'm going to start making him happy! You know . . . it's really not much fun hiding bikes and doing mean things.

Debbie: Oh, Bud, I'm so happy! Would you like to go with me to Sunday School?

Bud: Sure . . . ah . . . Debbie . . .

Debbie: Yes, Bud?

Bud: I think you are . . . wonderful!!

Debbie: *(Giggling)* Ah . . . Bud!

Honor Thy Mother*

by Tom deGraaf

Willie, His Sister Sally, Dad, Cool Charlie

Willie: *(Enters grumbling to himself)* Grumble, Grumble! Aw phooey! Phooey! Phoooooooey! Mom won't let me have a motorcycle. She says I'm too young. But I'm eight years old!

Sally: *(Enters—Hears Willie's last statement— Sarcastically)* Well congratulations Methuselah! Now what's all the grumbling about anyway? You look mean and sour enough to be Attila the Grapefruit.

Willie: *(Pouty)* Mom won't let me have a motorcycle. She says only guys like Evil KaNavel get to have motorcycles —cause they're nutty!

Sally: So you're in!?! I mean when it comes to nitwits- —You really shine brother.

Charlie: *(Enters as Sally says nitwit. Doesn't see Willie)* Hey Sally Baby! How ya doin' Chickie?

Sally: *(Coyly)* Cluck—Cluck *(Waves at him cutely)*

Charlie: *(Tries to change subject)* Uh, I heard you mention nitwit. Is your brother around?

Sally: He's right behind you and he's pouting because our mom won't let him have a motorcycle.

Charlie: But Willie, you're only eight years old—Still wet behind everything. You don't need a cycle. You're too young and ignorant to die.

Willie: Aw Phooey . . . Phoooooooey! Mom don't know what she's talking about.

Sally: *(Horrified)* Willie!! How could you say such a thing!?!

Charlie: That was not too cool man! Even Cool Charlie does not make discredulous remarks concerning his dear repreciated mother!

Willie: *(Still stewing)* Aw Phooey. I'm bugged off. Why can't Mom understand that I've got to have a Honda or I can't join the "SCREAMIN' WHEELIES"?

Sally: The Screamin' Wheelies? You don't mean that dead beat motorcycle club from across town? Yuky—Stinko!

Willie: *(Proudly)* Yep!

Sally: But those guys only have one motorcycle *(Laughs)* They all ride on it together! Plus they smell!

Willie: That's why I want my own cycle. *(Dreamily)* I'll be

Soooo Coooool! *(Gets pouty again)* That's why I'm mad at Mom!

Dad: *(Enters as Willie says he's mad at Mom)* Oh, So you're mad at your mother, huh Willie? And what for?

Willie: *(Shaking with fright)* HeeHee *(Shakes)*

Charlie: Hi, Mr. Weekers. Willie's mad at his mother because she won't let him have a motorcycle so he can join the Screamin' Wheelies.

Dad: Isn't that the motorcycle gang that rides around on one cycle?

Sally: Yep! And what a miserable bunch they are—They don't take baths!

Dad: I know!! This morning they drove by our house while I was mowing the lawn and it wilted before I could finish.

Willie: Aw Phooey . . .

Dad: Willie, I think you really do know that your mom is right, don't you? She is just trying to help you do what's best for you, and joining the Screamin' Wheelies certainly isn't.

Willie: Aw . . . I guess you're right Dad. I'm sorry I got mad at Mom. I guess I really don't need a cycle 'till I'm at least ten.

Dad: I know a Bible verse that we ought to all learn and remember about our moms. It says "Honor thy Mothers." (Ex. 20:12)

Charlie: Hey Mr. Weekers, do you think we could teach those kids out there *(In audience)* that verse? That's cool man!

Sally: Yeah Dad, let's all say it together!!

Dad: OK. Everybody repeat after me. *(They repeat the verse three or four times. Making sure it's learned.)*

Willie: Well, I'm not ever gonna say anything bad about Mom again!

Dad: *(Firmly)* I hope not Willie, because the rest of the verse says, "That thy days may be long in this earth!" Get my meanin'?

Willie: Yes, Dad. *(They all say bye to the kids and exit.)*

It Happened One Mother's Day*

by Tom deGraaf

Willie, Cool Charlie, Sally, Dad

Charlie: *(Enters)* Do-Do-Bop-I love my Mom-Beedly-Bob-a-Do-Yes I Do

Willie: *(Enters with Sally. Both are distressed)* Oh Cool Charlie, you've got to help us!

Sally: Oh please Cool Charlie, you've got to—if you don't, I'll just die! *(She starts to cry and cry) WaaaaWaaaa*

Willie: *(Looks at Sally and starts crying too)* Aaaa-WooWoo!

Charlie: *(Looks slowly at Willie and Sally who are crying, holding each other. Then he slowly looks at the audience)* OK . . . Shut up . . . I'll help!

Sally & Willie: *(Immediately stop crying, as if they hadn't cried at all)* You will?

Charlie: Yeah, Yeah. Now what can the Cool Charlie do for you two cry-persons?

Sally: Yesterday our family went skiing and when we got home last night, it was so late all the stores were closed. We could not buy our wonderful mom a Mother's Day present. She'll be crushed!

Willie: So will I. Dad gave me some money to get Mom something from him and I can't get that either! He's gonna kill me!

Charlie: Hold it everybody! The Cool Charlie is thinking'! I will come up with your typical genius-type idea to remedy this situation. So everyone QUIET! *(He holds his hands up to head and thinks—All is quiet for about fifteen seconds, then . . . Willie, who is watching Cool Charlie intently,*

suddenly hears a fly come buzzing into the room. Make buzzing sound. He watches it buzz around and around, make some sounds like a diving airplane, until it lands on the stage rail. He smacks his hand down on it and traps it. Cool Charlie slowly looks over at him. Willie then scoops up the fly and gluttonously eats it, licking his fingers as he finishes)*

Charlie: *(Matter-of-factly to the audience)* That was the most ill-mannered thing I have ever witnessed! *(Looks slowly over at Willie)* YOU couldn't even share that with me and your sister could you . . .?

Willie: *(Burps)*

Charlie: I have it! I have the answer to your problem!

Sally and Willie: Oh what, Cool Charlie!?! How can we get our mom a Mother's Day gift?

Charlie: *(Triumphantly)* I, Cool Charlie, will, through my underground connections, get your mother a very nice gift.

Sally and Willie: Hurray for Cool Charlie!!

Charlie: And, I will personally deliver it to her door for you . . . Classy, huh?

Sally: Oh thanks Cool Charlie!

Willie: How can I ever repay you?

Charlie: Just hang on to the next three or four praying mantises you find—I love those crunchy little devils! *(Licks fingers)*

(They exit)

Dad: *(Enters)* Now where in the world are those kids?

Willie — Sally!

Willie and Sally: *(Enter slowly–scared of Dad)* Hee Hee
. . .

Sally: Hi Dad, happy Father's Day!

Dad: Today is Mother's Day, Sally.

Sally: I know—*(Gulps)*—but I like you so much I want every day to be Father's Day!

Willie: Me too . . .

Dad: *(Knowingly)* All right, what'd you guys do? Forget to get Mom's present?

(Willie and Sally look at each other, then burst into tears—nodding their heads YES.)

Dad: Oh great. There goes my fishing trip next weekend!

Willie: But wait Dad, Cool Charlie said he'd get Mom some presents and even deliver them to her personally!

Sally: Yeah! Like Western Union.

Dad: *(Stricken)* You let Cool Charlie pick out Mom's presents!?!

Willie: *(Weakly)* The stores were closed. We had no choice.

Charlie: *(Comes up singing)* Beep-Bop-a-Do-And the Same to You . . . Oh hi Guys. Hi Mr. Weekers.

Sally: *(Excited)* What'd ya get Mom, Huh? What'd ya get her. Cool Charlie?

Charlie: Don't nobody worry! *(Confidently—triumphantly)* I got and personally delivered the best two presents a mother could want!

Dad: I hate to ask . . .

Sally: What'd ya get Cool Charlie, huh?

Cool: I got . . . are you ready for this? I got, from you two guys to your mom, the best gallon of perfume two dollars can buy! *(Sally and Willie faint away)* Corral No. 5!

Dad: *(Looks sickly at the audience)* Oh No . . .

Charlie: *(Proudly)* And to your . . . Now listen to this . . . To your wife from you, Mr. Weekers, I got her a matching end table and lamp with a picture of Arizona on it!

Dad: *(Looks up, faints, and keels over backwards.)*

Charlie: Now there's a family that loves their mom almost as much as I love mine!!

(To the audience): Happy Mother's Days girls! *(Waves, exits)*

———

Give Thanks

by Joan King

One, Two, Three

One: Look at all of those people. What are they doing?

Two: Shopping. They're Thanksgiving shopping.

One: Thanksgiving Shopping? Don't you mean Christmas shopping?

Two: No, they're Thanksgiving shopping. You see, Thanksgiving is only a few days away.

Three: What are they shopping for? Thanksgiving presents?

Two: No, you don't know anything, do you?

Three: Well, what are they shopping for?

Two: Turkeys, turkeys, turkeys.

One: Is that what Thanksgiving is all about?

Three: Yeah, you see, the Great Turkey visits all good boys and girls and brings them presents and puts them under the Thanksgiving tree.

Two: You have both got a lot to learn. Thanksgiving is the day set aside for everyone to thank God for all of their blessings.

Three: What kind of blessings?

Two: All blessings, but there is one special blessing many people forget to thank God for on Thanksgiving—that's the blessing sent to us through his Son, Jesus Christ.

Three: Why do people forget to thank God for his most special blessing?

Two: I don't know. I suppose that we get too involved in turkeys, Pilgrims, and all of the other symbols of Thanksgiving to remember why we should be so thankful. If God had not loved us enough to allow Jesus to die on the cross so that we might be forgiven for our sins, all of our other blessings would mean nothing. We should all remember this Thanksgiving to be extra grateful for God's greatest blessing.

One: Why don't we all listen to our friends sing a Thanksgiving song.

73

Section IV
GENERAL

My Friend, Watt

by Carroll Bryant Brown

Narrator, Watt, Oscar

Narrator: Once upon a time there were two bosom buddies—Oscar and Watt. While Watt was away in a small town, Lightsburg, he encountered a great truth which brightened and put a new perspective on his whole life. He couldn't wait to get back to Darksville, U.S.A. to share this great truth with his dear friend Oscar.

Watt: *(Enters whistling "Send the Light" or some current song or chorus about light. He is illuminated by lightbulb on his head.)* Hey Os-carrr, Os-carr, ole buddy, where are you?

Oscar: *(Enters slowly, sees the brightness of Watt, jumps back and covers his eyes. Slowly he looks up at his friend.)* Man, who zapped you? *(Looks at Oscar and acts like he is a real weird-o. Exits quickly and re-enters with sunglasses.)* Had to get my shades, man.

Watt: Well, do you like me? I got zapped over in Lightsburg. Now I see, and have the light! Praise the Lord!

Oscar: Well, cut if off, you nincompoop. What are you trying to do—ruin Darksville?

Watt: I can't cut it off. But, don't worry, ole pal. *(Puts arm around Oscar)* What's mine is yours. You can't help it that you're not so bright!

Oscar: Oh! No, thanks. I think it's time to split. So long. *(Watt drops his head)* Oh, Watt?

Watt: *(Turns anxiously)* Uhm?

Oscar: I just got one thing to say.

Watt: What Oscar?

Oscar: The light couldn't be that crucial; why not put it under a bushel? Ha ha! *(Watt exits, and Oscar turns to audience.)* Some guys would do anything for a laugh! *(Exit)* *(Music interlude)*

Oscar: *(Enters and drops coin)* Doggone it! My last quarter! Now where did that stupid coin go? I wish I could see to find it. *(Watt enters, lights brighten)* Wow! Who turned on the lights? Here it is. Oh boy! *(Turns and sees Watt.)*

Watt: Hi, ya, Oscar. Still mad at me!

Occar: *(Looks at Watt, then at coin.)* Mad? Who me? Well, heck no, ole buddy! You know what? *(Hugs friend)*

Watt: What Oscar?

Oscar: It's kinda nice having such a bright friend!

Watt: *(Acts bashful)* Aw, great day! *(Exit hugging)* *(Several puppets sing chorus about light)*

The Summer Slump*

by Tom deGraaf

Willie, Sally, Cool Charlie, Dad

Sally: *(Enters with Willie. They are chatting)* I don't understand it.

Willie: You don't understand what?

Sally: We had 22 people in Sunday School last Sunday.

Willie: Sooo?

Sally: Willie you know good and well that we usually have about 450 people in Sunday School! I can never figure out why our attendance always takes a nose-dive when summer comes!

Willie: I didn't notice.

Sally: *(Irritated)* We dropped from 450 down to 22 in one week and you didn't notice? What are you? A terminal "out-to-lunch" case? How could you not notice nobody was there?!!?

Willie: Simple. I wasn't there last week either.

Sally: You weren't there?!!? I thought you went with Dad and I went with Mom?

Willie: (*Sheepishly*) . . . Me and Dad went fishin' instead.

Sally: (*Draws in breath*) Wait till I tell Mom!!! You guys ditched!

Charlie: (*Enters, jiving*) Bebop-a-doo-doo. Hey Sally! What-cha gonna tell your mom? Willie what'd you do, you sly devil.

Sally: (*Points to Willie*) That backsliding brother of mine ditched church last week to go fishing!

Charlie: (*Horrified*) You did that Willie!??? You went fishing?!?

Willie: Yep . . .

Charlie: (*To Sally*) Hasn't he seen Jaws yet?

Sally: (*Irritated*) Cool Charlie you're a big help! I'm trying to figure out why Willie and 400 other people skipped church last Sunday and you're worried about some dumb movie! (*Settles down*) . . . Now, we have got to get to the bottom of this problem. I just know the preacher is sick about it, and there's no telling how God is taking it. We've got to find out why church attendance slumps during the summer!

Charlie: (*Confidently*) Have no fear, Cool Charlie is here with the answer! I have just come up with the perfect plan.

Willie: What is it Cool Charlie? Do we put everybody in the church under surveillance? I'll help—My eyes are real good! (*Points to eyes*) As a matter of fact, I drink carrot juice to strengthen my eyes . . . The only thing . . . is now I have trouble sleeping—I see through my eyelids!

Sally: (*Menacingly*) One more joke like that and you'll be seeing through a clump of stars!! (*Holds up fist*) Understand??

Charlie: OK you two—Cool it! Now here's my idea for solving the slump mystery. (*All three put their heads together and whisper back and forth*) OK—Let's try it out Sunday. (*All exit, Dad enters*)

Dad: Oh hi folks. Have you seen Willie and Sally? Well I've been looking all over for them because they've got some chores to do at home and if they don't do them soon, their mother will make me do 'em! . . . (*Looks around*) . . . Well, if you see those kids you tell 'em I'm looking for them and to come home. I'm going now—Bye. (*Exits*)

Willie: (*Willie, Sally, and Cool Charlie enter talking to each other. They are excited*) Hey Cool Charlie, that is a great idea!

Sally: Yeah! I'll bet we'll have 5,000 people in Sunday School this coming Sunday if we follow your plan to beat the summer slump!

Charlie: (*Triumphantly*) Don't worry about a thing. We may even have 389!!

Willie: (*Confidentially*) Uh Cool Charlie, (*Loud whisper*) 389 is less than 5,000.

Charlie: (*Embarrassed*) It is? Well, I meant 5,000!

Sally: Hurray for Cool Charlie!! I can hardly wait for Sunday.

Willie: Me either!

(*They all exit. Pause ten seconds–Then all enter walking slowly—Dejected*)

Dad: Well I hope you kids learned a lesson from this little adventure of yours . . .

Kids: (*Looking sheepishly at each other—In unison*) We did! . . .

Dad: What ever made you kids think that you could actually get away with a stunt like you tried to pull this morning at church?

Sally: We just thought we could help get our church attendance out of the summer slump . . .

Dad: That's a noble thought Dear, but how could you ever think of doing it by advertising free root beer to everyone who came?!? I mean that is not a standard practice for promoting church attendance. And whose idea was it to give away a door prize to the first 100 members to show up?

Willie: It was mine.

Dad: And I'll bet it was Sally's idea to "pack a pew and win a pizza"?

Charlie: . . . It was mine Mr. Weekers.

Dad: Well I hope you've all learned a lesson.

Willie: We have! It cost us a fortune to give away all that root beer and pizza—Not to mention the door prizes and bobbing for apples. (*Grabs mouth*) Didn't mean to tell about the apples.

Dad: Bobbing for apples? Oh no—You didn't . . .

Sally: (*Nods her head yes*) We had it in the baptistry. The preacher wiped us out though. He got the advantage because he had his waders on, and he ate every single apple!

Dad: (*Looks skyward—shakes his head slowly—Then looks at kids*) And how many people did we have in Sunday School as a result of your . . . attendance campaign?

Charlie: Twenty-two, the same as the Sunday before.

Dad: (*Seriously*) Do you know what that tells me? It says to me that even though we may be concerned about our attendance during the summer, attendance gimmicks aren't really going to solve our slump, and do you know why?

Kids: (*In unison*) No.

Dad: Because people need their vacation times. Our members work hard all year long and then we gripe at them for taking their hard-earned two or three weeks vacation time.

Now I'll grant you that it seems like a disaster area around here sometimes because so many are gone, but summer is the only time they can go. Look at our church offerings. They haven't gone down much at all, and do you know why?

Kids: *(In unison)* No.

Dad: Because our members are still faithful to their church's ministry even though they may not be here. They are still sending in their tithes. Now if you want to see a church that's in trouble, it's one whose attendance and giving is down. That's a church with problems.

Charlie: So you're saying our church is still strong??

Dad: Sure it is! And just as soon as summer is over and each family has finished taking its turn at vacationing, we'll be more rested and stronger than ever! So kids—please—no more unauthorized attendance drives—OK?

Kids: *(In unison)* O—K!

Sally: But you have to promise us something too!

Dad: What's that dear?

Sally: No more unauthorized fishing trips like you and Willie took last Sunday. Do it on your two-week vacation time like everybody else!

Dad: Yes Dear. *(They all leave)*

---

*Reprinted from *California Puppets*, Mill Valley, California. © Copyright, 1975. Used by permission.

The First Day of Summer*

by Tom deGraaf

Willie, Sally, Cool Charlie, Sammy Shnirk (New Kid)

Willie: *(Enters wearing a beach hat, with a towel around his neck)* Doo-Bop-Adoo-doo—Hot Fun In The Summer Time. Doo-Bop-Shuwa . . .

Sally: *(Enters Slaps Willie on the back)* Hi Willie!!

Willie: YeeOooww!! Ooo Ouch . . . Pain . . . Ouch . . . Discomfort!

Sally: What'd I do wrong?

Willie: You slapped me right on my sunburn!

Sally: Sorry Willie, I must have got excited when I saw you—. I've never seen a red turkey before! A Haw Haw How! *(Slaps him on the back again)*

Willie: OOOwweee! Stop that! . . . Oh Ouch! May a grape jellyfish tentacle your body!

Charlie: *(Enters jiving, wearing sunglasses, towel around neck)* Hey Guys, what's happening!? The Cool Charlie is here!

Sally: Cool Charlie! Hey, Look at Willie . . . He got a sunburn!

Charlie: *(Looks at Willie)* Hey Willie, what's with the two hand marks on your back? . . . You get a tatoo?

Willie: Oooo . . . No . . . Sally wacked me on my sunburn.

Sally: Be thankful Flaming Turkey . . . If it wasn't for a sunburn you wouldn't have a body!

Charlie: I don't mean to interrupt you two—But what ya got goin' for the summer?

Sally: What do you mean?

Charlie: Well we're out of school. What do you plan to do for the next three months? I'm thinkin' about goin' off to summer camp the whole time. There's this place up in the mountains called Camp Ivyitchy that's got a lake and beach and everything . . .

Willie: *(Looks at Sally)* Do they allow girls?

Charlie: Yep!

Willie: *(Still Looking at Sally)* That let's you out! A Haw Haw Haw!

Sally: *(Slaps Willie on the back again. He yelps and falls down behind stage. Sally yells down)* Real cute Tomato Face!

Sam: *(Enters)* Hi Sally. Hi Cool Charlie!

Charlie: Hey! It's Sammy Shnirk, the new kid at church! How ya doin' Sammy Baby?

Sam: OK, Mr. Cool Charlie! Hey you look like you're goin' to the beach!

Sally: We was just tryin' to figure out what to do this summer . . . Cool Charlie's thinkin' about spending the

77

entire summer up at Camp Ivyitchy. I'm trying' to decide if me and Willie are goin' there too.

Willie: *(Comes up moaning)* Ooooo . . .

Sam: *(Excited)* Hi Willie!! *(Slaps Willie on the back)*

Willie: *(Doesn't move. Looks at Sammy. Slowly turns and looks at the audience. Yells, keels over backwards)*

Sally: Well, at least I'm looking for something to do this summer . . .

Sam: Hey wait a minute . . . Do you mean to say that you and Willie and Cool Charlie leave for the whole summer?

Sally: Most of it.

Sam: But what about going to church and Sunday School and to our Youth Choir? Don't you go??

Charlie: *(Looks at Sally)* Uh, Listen Sammy—you're new at our church—Right?

Sam: Right!

Charlie: Well, we just got a thing here at our church where almost everybody leaves for the summer. I mean it's as Baptist as taking collections.

Sam: But doesn't everyone's leaving hurt the church? How can it keep going the way it's supposed to?

Sally: *(Looks at Cool Charlie. They shrug their shoulders)*

Willie: *(Comes back up—holding a white flag with a red cross on it, in shock)* Peace . . . Again I say peace.

Sam: Hey Willie, Sally and Cool Charlie says you guys are going away from church for the entire summer. Do you really think that's right? I know I'm just new at your church,

but it doesn't seem right to me that you guys just leave church all summer.

Willie: *(Still in shock. Hasn't heard Sam)* Dearly Beloved, I am gathered here together in memory of my back.

Sally: *(Grabs his flag and bonks him on the head with it)* Willie, how dare you say you're going away for the summer and leave the church. Cool Charlie and I are simply appalled at your lack of dedication—Aren't we Cool Charlie!?!!

Charlie: Yeah, Man! That's no way to act Willie. I'm ashamed of you. Wanting to run off to summer camp and miss church and Youth Choir!

Willie: *(Still in shock)* Why do I feel like an accident stuck on instant replay?

Sally: Come on you guys. Let's go down to the church and ask the preacher what we can do this summer to help out at church!

(They all leave, excited, except Willie, who is still standing, staring in shock)

Willie: *(Stands for a moment. Looks straight ahead. Hears a bee come buzzing around. Buzzing noise–Finally the bee lights on his shoulder. Willie slowly looks toward it, then back at the audience. Then back at the bee. Takes a mighty swing and hits his own shoulder)* Aaaarrgghh! My SUNBURN! *(Faints off stage, backwards)*

The Happy Weirdo

by Sarah Walton Miller

Two Puppets

One: Hi, there, Neighbor! Where are you off to, all dressed up?

Two: The church down the street. I'm a new member there.

One: So someone told me. Well, it's everyone to his own liking. Say, this isn't Sunday.

Two: I want to tell someone in charge there that I can sing and teach.

One: Well, lah-d-dah! Toot my horn!

Two: It isn't like that at all.

One: Well it sounds like that to me. "Hey, look at me! I'm a great singer and I can teach up a storm! You're sure lucky to have me for a member!"

Two: In the first place I'm not a great singer. Just a pretty good one.

One: Wow! Listen to that!

Two: And in the second place I am a pretty fair teacher of teenagers. I understand and like them and they soon take to me.

One: Brotherrrr! Do you remember the oldie? "He who tooteth not his own horn, the same shall not be tooted?" Listen to you! Wow! Bragging!

Two: I don't think of it as bragging. I think of it as honesty. After all, I know better than anyone what I can do and how well I can do it. Shall I lie in false modesty and say I can't sing a note and don't know anything about the Bible? . . . Shall I?

One: Uh—no, not that. But, Neighbor, there is such a thing as humility and modesty.

Two: Overworked humility can be a sin. Somewhere in the Bible there ought to be a Scripture that says, "The Lord loveth a cheerful volunteer!"

One: Aw, now! Listen—wouldn't it look better to wait until someone finds out, and let them tell the pastor. Then eventually—

Two: I could sit there and die of old age! I'm off to tell someone I can sing and I can teach! 'Bye, now. *(Two exits)*

One: *(Calling after)* Don't be disappointed if they think you're a weirdo!

Youth Workers' Oath*

by Tom deGraaf

Dad, Willie, Sally

Dad: *(Enters dejectedly carrying a large book entitled Working with Youth)* Oh phooey! I don't know why I even try anymore. That silly youth group never notices or appreciates a thing I do for them. *(Pause)* Take last week just for instance. I took the whole youth group to the park as a part of our study on God's creations. I figured it would do the kids some good to get close to nature for a while and see God's handiwork. Well, the only thing they got close to was Happy Harvey's Hot Dog Stand! Cleaned him out. I don't know why I even try anymore. Those kids don't want to learn or appreciate anything. I might as well give up.

Sally: *(Enters with Willie. Both have heard Dad's remark)* What'sa matter Dad? You sound degenerate.

Dad: Despondent maybe. Degenerate—NO.

Willie: What happened Dad? Was it bad? Are you hurt? Is it your hernia again!

Dad: No Son. It's not that . . . It's the youth group.

Sally: That's worse isn't it?

Dad: Well, sometimes . . .

Willie: What's the problem Dad? Are those older kids kissing again?

Dad: Yes, but that's not the main problem.

Sally: *(Triumphant)* I got it! You're still upset about that trip to the park when all the youth ditched your nature study and ended up at Happy Harvey's Hot Dog Stand! Right??

Dad: Yeah, that's part of it. You see kids, I don't think the youth group appreciates one thing I do. And I really do try! I mean I do the best I can to teach those kids.

Sally: I know Dad. It was really swell of you when you took 'em all on that beach party.

Willie: *(Trying to cheer Dad up)* Yeah! It was Dad! Those youth had a great time swimming and building sand castles!!

Dad: They were supposed to be sharing and witnessing.

Willie: Oh . . .

Dad: You know the thing that really hurts me the most is the way our new youth project is going.

Sally: What is it?

Dad: Well, I thought it would be good if our youth would start doing some visiting this month. That way, maybe we could get back some of the kids who have drifted away.

Willie: Hey! That sounds like a great idea.

Sally: Yeah! Kids like to go see their friends. Drive around together. Stuff like that. I'll bet the youth group really went for that visitation idea!

Dad: They think it stinks. All they want to do is cruise and get Cokes. I give up.

Sally: *(Puts arm around Dad)* Dad, I know your feelings are hurt. You're trying to do good as a youth worker and a lot of people in our church do appreciate it. Why I've heard several people say that you are the most dedicated worker we've got!

Willie: Who said that? I didn't hear anybody say that!

Sally: *(Annoyed)* Quiet dummy! You're about as tactful as stomach cramps! Anyway, I think it's wonderful what you're trying to do with the youth. I also know that you didn't feel like you're getting much accomplished with them, but you are. You would probably be surprised at how much good you are actually doing, even if you can't really see it now.

Willie: Yeah Dad! Those kids are picking up more than you think. It's just that they're not showing it much.

Dad: Maybe so.

Sally: Sure! Hey Dad! I'll bet you've even forgotten the "Youth Worker's Oath!"

Dad: Huh?

Sally: Remember? You told it to us! The "Youth Worker's Oath."

Dad: I guess I did forget it—But thanks for reminding me! Boy if it wasn't for that verse I don't know how I'd ever survive! Well, I've got to go kids. The Youth group is waiting for me to go bowling with them tonight. I only hope they don't fill the ball holes with white glue again! See you guys at home—Bye! *(He exits)*

Sally: Oh Willie, wasn't it great to see Dad get encouraged again about working with the youth?

Willie: Yeah—I thought he was going to give up there for a while. Hey, what was that "Youth Worker's Oath" you were talking about anyway? It sure did the trick for Dad.

Sally: Oh it's a verse from Galatians—chapter 6, verse 9 that says "And let us not get tired of doing what is right, for after a while we will reap a harvest of blessing if we don't get discouraged and give up."

Willie: I sure hope Dad keeps remembering that verse when we get old enough to be in the youth group!

Sally: That's for sure! If Dad can put up with us, he's in for some pretty heavy blessings!

Willie: For sure! *(They laugh and exit)*

God's Rainbow

by Sarah Walton Miller

Black, White

Black: Man, I'm sure tired of winter. Same old thing every day. School and home. School and home.

White: Me, too. But it ain't long till spring. Good old spring! Just thinking of spring makes my skin twitch.

Black: Aw, that's the itchy wool you've got on.

White: Maybe. Well, then, tell me how do you spell blue?

Black: Blue? What kinda word is blue?

White: Makes no never mind what kind it is. How do you spell it?

Black: Well, it oughta start with a "b" I think. Buh-buh-blue-see? That's a "b" sound I'm sure. Why do you want to spell blue?

White: Well, it's spring, ain't it?

Black: Just almost.

White: Anyway soon there'll be summer, and I can go swimming, and when I jump in I want to say blue!

Black: Man, you are the most. Can't you just say it without spelling it out?

White: *(Marveling)* I never thought of that.

Black: Man, you better get yourself together and live through spring first. Don't worry about summer. Or swimming.

White: Oh, yeah? I felt a twig yesterday and it had bumps. The leaves are just busting to get out. Come to think of it, I can't decide if I like green leaves, like the spring, or red leaves like the fall.

Black: Don't talk about leaves. Man, before Christmas, I raked ten zillion, zillion leaves.

White: They all start out green. Wonder why they turn red and orange and yellow?

Black: Cause God made 'em that way, is why . . . I wonder what color is God?

White: I dunno for sure. One time I went to a picture museum.

Black: Picture museum?

White: Yeah, a big building with nothing in it but pictures.

Black: Nothing but pictures?

White: That's all. There was a Chinese picture of Jesus and he looked yellow. Then there was an Indian picture of Jesus and he looked red. And there was an African picture of him and he looked black. What do you think of that?

Black: *(Thinking)* Yeah? Hey! Maybe God is every color!

White: Like a rainbow?

Black: *(Thinking of the two of them)* Even black and white.

White: *(Happily)* Of course black and white. You are right. Didn't he say we were brothers in Christ?

Black: *(Laughing)* Yeah, man! Wow! Won't my mom be surprised when I bring you home and say, "Look, Mom! Here's another one of our kids!"

(Exit, laughing)

When Wilbur Did His Thing

by Sarah Walton Miller

Wilbur, Prunella

Wilbur: *(Loudly)* Prunella! I'm here! Let's go to the church . . . Prunella! Come out, wherever you are. I'm waiting! *(Prunella enters, dismayed at the sight of him)*

Prunella: Wilbur! Whatever has happened to you?

Wilbur: *(In a deep voice)* Don't call me Wilbur! Call me Slash, Babe!

Prunella: Slash? Wilbur Hopple, have you lost your mind? Look at that hat—and your hair! What's that thing you've got on?

Wilbur: *(Proudly)* This is my costume, Babe. Like it?

Prunella: Not much! You know what you look like? You look like a—a hippie! You smell like one, too!

Wilbur: *(Happily)* Yeah. Let's go, Babe. Give the folks at church a gander.

Prunella: *(Firmly)* I'm not going one step with you looking like that and smelling so bad.

Wilbur: *(Wheedling)* Aw, Babe, I'm just doing my thing.

Prunella: Well, you just go do it somewhere else!

Wilbur: Aw, now, Babe—

Prunella: Stop calling me Babe!

Wilbur: Just my new way of talking. This is the new *me*. You'll get used to it!

Prunella: Oh, no, I won't, Wilbur Hoople! Go away!

Wilbur: *(Annoyed)* Now look here! We're supposed to go to the church—rap session or something.

Prunella: How much do you think we'd get done with you sitting there looking and smelling like that? You'd break it all up. No!

Wilbur: But we have a date!

Prunella: *(Coldly)* I had a friend named Wilbur Hoople. Not a—hippie called Slash, *(Sniffs loudly)* who doesn't smell very good.

Wilbur: *(Annoyed)* Get with it, Babe! No bathing—that's the scene.

Prunella: *(Angrily)* Well, scene it somewhere I can't smell you! Why you picked this out to model after—

Wilbur: Now listen here, Prunella, you don't understand—

Prunella: *(Sharply)* Oh, yes, I do! You're trying to do "your thing"—

Wilbur: That's it!

Prunella: But your thing I don't like! Now I'm going to do my thing. I'm going to the church all by myself, Wilbur Hoople.

Wilbur: Then you just do it! That's your loss, Babe!

Prunella: Not in my book. Not a loss at all.

Wilbur: Okay, okay! I can get along without you.

Prunella: Fine! Do that.

Wilbur: I can find lots of girls—

Prunella: More's the pity!

Wilbur: They'll like my costume!

Prunella: Poor things.

Wilbur: I'm leaving!

Prunella: Go right ahead. Good-bye. *(A pause. WILBUR is worried)*

Wilbur: Prunella? . . . Prunella, does your good-bye mean—good-bye?

Prunella: Absolutely!

Wilbur: *(Puzzled)* Why? Why won't you take me as I am?

Prunella: Wilbur, this isn't the real you. This is a loud, rude, dirty, unkempt lout!

Wilbur: *(Sneeringly)* So the people at church won't like me because I'm different!

Prunella: No, Wilbur. What they won't like is your not being yourself—trying to be something just to annoy people.

Wilbur: . . . Is that how it looks, Prunella?

Prunella: Yes.

Wilbur: I just wanted to do my thing.

Prunella: Even when your thing annoys everyone else trying to do their thing? I think you're trying to grow up—to be a free person, all together.

Wilbur: Right!

Prunella: Don't you see this is the wrong way? Breaking down standards just to break down standards isn't very constructive. Think it over.

Wilbur: *(Silence, then)* Prunella, if I go change clothes—

Prunella: And bathe! And cut your hair!

Wilbur: And bathe. And cut—a little hair.

Prunella: All right.

Wilbur: Will you go with me then, Prunella?

Prunella: Yes, Wilbur.

Wilbur: *(Happily)* You will? Oh, Prunella, wait right here! I'll get rid of this stuff quick! *(He starts off. Then she calls out)*

Prunella: Oh—Wilbur?

Wilbur: Yes?

Prunella: Let me have that thing you're wearing. I was just thinking—if I took off that gaudy fringe—it's just the thing to wear with my new slacks!

Wilbur: Aw-w-w! *(He leaves. She follows, calling out)*

Prunella: Did you hear me, Wilbur? Wilburrrrr! *(They are gone)*

I'm a Puppet

by Sarah Walton Miller

One, Two

(One enters, wailing loudly. Two enters after a pause and listens to him)

One: *(Wailing)* Ooooh, ooooh! I am a puppet! It's awful to be a puppet! It's terrible to be a puppet! Woe is me! I am only a puppet!

Two: Why are you carrying on this way, you silly puppet?

One: That's it! Ooooh, ooooh! I am a puppet. It's awful to be a puppet! It's terrible to be a puppet! Woe is me! I am only a puppet!

Two: What's so bad about being a puppet?

One: *(Wailing)* What's so bad? I'll tell you what's so bad! I never can say what I think! A person always has to speak for me. That's what's so bad!

Two: What would you say if you could?

One: I don't know! But I'd say something! I don't want to be a puppet.

Two: If you weren't a puppet, what would you want to be?

One: *(Still wailing)* The person, that's who! Then I could speak for myself all the time. O happy day!

Two: Uh-huh. Well then I suppose you want to have drippy miserable colds?

One: *(Surprised)* Certainly not! What a silly question.

Two: People do. How about taking shots, and having headaches, and worrying about a job?

One: *(Crossly)* I don't want to do that.

Two: People do. They do all these things and more. A puppet never has to be concerned about colds, or jobs, or taxes, or chores, or any of these things.

One: *(Thoughtfully)* That's true. I don't, do I? Are you sure people have all those things to put up with? You're not just making it up?

Two: No, It's the truth. But you'll find out since you want to be a person.

One: *(Hedging)* Well-uh-well, I did. But maybe I'd better think about it.

Two: Oh? Well, make up your mind.

One: Don't rush me! I'm going off to think a while. *(One exits)*

Two: The truth is no person would want to be a puppet either. He'll realize soon that being the best of whatever you are —well, you can't beat that, can you? *(Two leaves)*

Willie Blows a Test*

by Tom deGraaf

Youth Director, Willie, Sally, Dad

Youth Director: As Youth Director of our church, I feel it my duty to help you young people in any way I can. Since school has started again, it's come to my attention that though physically your bodies show up there, mentally most of you are still on vacation! I feel it's my obligation, to point out the perils of such a situation. And I think of no better way to do this than to present a sad-but-true-story about two back-to-schoolers who find themselves in precisely this position.

Willie: *(Enters cautiously—looks all round to make sure he's alone—Bows head and covers eyes)* Dear Lord don't let anybody find out about that test I flunked. I know it was my fault, but please try and let it go this time. Amen. *(Starts to get up, then remembers)* And please make Sally stop punching me . . . By the way, I've mentioned this before . . . Amen.

Sally: *(Enters)* Hi Willie! How was your first week of school?

Willie: Oh, . . . It was OK. My teacher said I show a lot of potential. She said I might even become a great intellectual

82

someday. What do you think? Do you think it's too soon to tell?

Sally: I think your teacher has gone fruit in the head. Besides, I just heard from Rita Frumpstead that you flunked your first math test. What do you have to say about that Mister Einstein?

Willie: *(Scared)* Don't tell Dad!! He'll kill me! Worse yet, he'll ground me from going to the football game next weekend! *(Pleads)* Sally, please don't tell Dad OK? Please?

Sally: *(Teasingly)* What's it worth to you, turkey?

Willie: Anything! I'll give you anything I've got— Everything I've got!! You can have my most valuable possessions!

Sally: You think I accept junk? I've seen the stuff in your room and it reminds me of Fred Sanford's throw-aways!

Dad: *(Enters, unaware of situation)* Hi kids!

Sally: Hi Dad! Willie flunked his first math test!

Willie: *(Horrified)* Aaaaarrrighh! *(Faints)*

Dad: What'sa matter with your brother!

Sally: He overtaxed his intellect, perplexed his mental poise . . .

Dad: What??

Sally: His brain went bananas. Haw Haw Haw! He's mad 'cause I told on him.

Dad: Willie, come here. We've got something to talk about!

Willie: *(Staggers up)* Dad, I'm sorry! I didn't mean to flunk—Honest! It wasn't all my fault.

Sally: *(Bratty)* Rita Frumpstead said part of the reason for Willie flunking was he didn't write legibly.

Willie: But if I do—the teacher'll know I can't spell either!

Dad: Willie, it seems like we've got a serious problem here. Now . . . Why did you flunk your math test?

Willie: I don't know . . . Maybe I'm under stress or something. Maybe I'm suffering at the borderline of insanity and genius . . .

Sally: More like the borderline of partial ineptitude and total vacancy!

Dad: Now that's enough Sally! Let Willie speak for himself. *(Puts arm around Willie)* Well, Son, I know this hasn't been a very good day for you. It's embarrassing to flunk a test and have the whole world find out about it. I know, I was young once.

Sally: You were?

Dad: *(Matter of factly)* You're grounded! *(To Willie)* As I was saying, I had my problems too, Son. But I overcame them by studying harder.

Willie: . . . I guess that's what I need to do then Dad. I need to study harder.

Dad: That's my boy! You don't want to turn out like that bunch—Do you? *(Points to audience)*

Willie: Well, I don't think so . . .

Dad: OK then. You get up to your room and hit the books. I want you to make an ''A'' on your next test!

Willie: An ''A''?!?

Dad: You can do it Son! I have faith and confidence that you'll make an ''A'' on your very next test!

Willie: There's no way . . .

Dad: Besides, you're grounded until you do. Now hit the books Son.

Sally: *(Laughs at Willie as he leaves)* Haw Haw . . . You're grounded too you turkey! Haw Haw.

Dad: Sally! *(She stops laughing)* You have a very special problem that we need to talk about right now!

Sally: Hee Hee. What's that Daddy?

Dad: I wasn't going to say anything, but I got a note from your teacher yesterday . . .

Sally: *(Scared)* Oh really? What'd she say?

Dad: Your teacher said that during a true-false examination the other day she saw you flipping a coin! Sally, is that any way to choose answers on a true-false test? Flipping a coin?

Sally: But Dad! I wasn't choosing my answers. I was rechecking them!!! I learned that from *(Youth in audience)!*

Dad: Sally, get up to your room and hit the books! *(She exits)* I don't know if these kids of mine will ever learn!! There's only one way to pass a test and that's good hard study. Yes Siree, Good Hard Study!

Sally and Willie: *(Both enter, carrying homework papers)*

Willie: Dad can you help me with this math problem? I think my hypotenuse is in the wrong place! Will you . . .?

Sally: Dad, Willie ripped my rhombus! *(Cries loudly)* Waaaaaa! *(Holds up ripped paper)*

Willie: *(Yells)* I did not! She just writes heavy!

Dad: *(Exasperated)* Quiet! *(Kids are immediately quiet)* Willie I don't even know what your hypotenuse is, let alone where it is. And Sally I'm sorry about your rhombus . . .

Willie: But aren't you gonna help us with our homework?

Sally: Yeah! I don't know if this answer is right or wrong!

Dad: Sally, why don't you go . . . flip a coin. *(She exits)* Willie, why don't you go ask your mother. *(He exits)* *(Looks up)* Dear God—I've mentioned this before. *(Faints)*

Inchworm

by Joan King

Henrietta, Miss Snickle, Alfred, Farmer Brown

SCENE I

(Henrietta enters mumbling to herself)

Henrietta: Oh, hi there. Did you hear about Alfred the Inchworm? He's my boyfriend! *(Giggles)* I'm sad because Alfred dropped out of school today. He thinks he is a mathematical genius and he told Miss Snickle, our teacher, that he could become another Albert Einstein if given the chance. So Miss Snickle gave him a compass and a slide rule and told him he could go out into the world and prove it. And now Alfred's gone and I'll never see him again. Whaa! *(She starts crying)*

Miss Snickle: Henrietta, what's the matter with you?

Henrietta: Oh, Miss Snickle. Alfred has dropped out of school and has a job measuring Farmer Brown's marigold plants. I'll never see him again. Whaa!

Miss Snickle: Henrietta, please stop crying. Come with me and help dust the erasers. I hope Alfred will decide to come back to school too.

Henrietta: I hope so, but I'm afraid he'll never come back.

(They exit)

SCENE II

Alfred: . . . five and five are ten, and six and six are twelve, and . . . Oh, hi there, people. I'm Alfred. I'm a genius. I'm so smart that I don't need to go to school. I don't need anybody's help to get along in life. I'm self-sufficient. Self-sufficient—that's me.

Henrietta: Hello, Alfred.

Alfred: Hi, Henrietta. I've got a new job. Farmer Brown needed someone to measure his crops to see if they're tall enough to harvest. I guess he heard about how smart I am. He gave me the job! I'm already well on the way to becoming a millionaire. Why he pays fifty cents an hour!

Henrietta: That sounds wonderful, Alfred. But I wish you were back in school. I certainly miss you.

Alfred: I'll never need school or anybody. I'm self-sufficient! I've got to get to work now. *(They exit)*

SCENE III

(Flowers appear. Song begins. Original words to Inchworm, first verse. See end of script.)

Alfred: Where did I put that compass? And my slide rule is gone. Oh, dear. What am I going to do? Did anybody see my slide rule?

Farmer Brown: Alfred, have you not finished yet?

Alfred: No, sir. I seem to have lost my compass and slide rule.

Farmer Brown: I suppose I am just going to have to get a more reliable inchworm to work on my farm.

Alfred: Oh please, sir. I'll finish. Just as soon as I find my slide rule.

Farmer Brown: I'm sorry, Alfred. But I'm afraid I'll have to hire someone else. *(Alfred is left alone)*

Alfred: I'm a failure. I've lost my compass and slide rule —and my job. What am I going to do? *(Henrietta enters)*

Henrietta: Alfred, what's wrong? Why are you so sad?

Alfred: I'm a failure—a total failure. What am I going to do?

Henrietta: You could come back to school.

Alred: After the way I acted? Oh, no. Miss Snickle would never let me in class again.

Henrietta: Oh, yes she would, Alfred. Because you're a prodigal student. Sort of like the prodigal son Miss Snickle told us about. Your self-reliance was not bad until it made you reject all authority. I'm afraid this is what you did, Alfred.

Alfred: Yes, now I know that, and I am sorry. Do you think Miss Snickle will let me return to her class the way the prodigal son's father allowed him to return? And do you think the Lord will forgive me of all my sins?

Henrietta: Yes, Alfred. Miss Snickle wants you to come back to school, and the Lord will always forgive us of our sins if we only ask him.

You and I have sinned,
All have fallen short,
Short of God's glory.
Yet he will forgive us of our sins.

Inchworm, Inchworm, you and I and all have sinned,
But we can find perfect peace by turning to the Lord.
Inchworm, Inchworm, I'm so glad that you have seen
Just how happy we can be by following God's Word.

Freedom Is . . .

by Sarah Walton Miller

Two Puppets

One: Hurrah! Wowee! I'm free! I'm free! Listen everybody!

Two: I *hear* you. You're free. So what?

One: Man, don't you understand? I'm free. I can do what I want and say what I want. That's reason to shout. I am free!

Two: Uh-huh. Within limits.

One: Ha! What limits? I'm free to do what I want! See this trash? *(Pick up basket)* I can dump it if I want to! *(Does so)*

Two: *(Commanding)* Pick it up!

One: Oh, no! I'm free!

Two: So am I! This is my yard. If you don't pick it up, I'll bop you on the nose.

One: *(Indignantly):* You can't do that!

Two: Watch me. Pick it up . . . Go on!

One: Aww. *(Either picks up trash or brushes it off)* Okayyyy! . . . Now are you satisfied?

Two: Yes. So long as your freedom doesn't mess up my yard.

One: You're a terrible neighbor! I ought to write a letter to the editor of the paper about you.

Two: He wouldn't print it. Nothing you say would interest anyone.

One: Oh, no? What if I say anyone who doesn't stand for freedom can't be a good American? For all I know you could be a member of a—a subversive group! Yeah, maybe even a spy! A menace to the good of the nation! A traitor who doesn't believe in freedom!

Two: *(Calmly)* Go ahead. If you *say* it, I'll sue you for slander. If you print it, I'll sue you for libel.

One: *(Indignantly)* You can't do that! I'm free!

Two: Just try me.

One: *(Plaintively)* How can I be free if I can't do what I want and say what I want?

Two: Don't be stupid. You can be as free as you like—so long as you don't take my freedom.

One: *(Puzzled)* What's that?

Two: That's the limit. Your freedom ends where mine begins.

One: What does that mean?

Two: It means you can't throw your trash in my yard, and you can't call me a traitor and damage my reputation.

One: That's my freedom?

Two: That's it.

One: Then what good is it?

Two: Well, it works both ways. *I* can't throw trash in your yard, and I can't slander or libel you.

One: *(Thinking. Pleased)* Yeah . . . Yeah! I am free, aren't I? Sure, man! I'm free!

Culture Shock

by Carroll Bryant Brown

Missionary Mark, Stewardess, Akumoah, 2 Porters

Stewardess: Flight 219 will land in Ghana in approximately five minutes. Please fasten your seat belt and observe the no-smoking sign. The temperature in Kumasi, Ghana is 115 degrees in the shade.

(African music)

Missionary Mark: *(Enters dressed as a tourist with flight bag and camera. Announcements blurt over the PA system)* Gee, I wonder what happened to everyone? I thought the missionaries would be here with a band to meet me. Well, I guess I'll try to find my bags. *(Porter enters)* Uh, pardon me sir. I was looking for my luggage—from Flight 219.

Porter Number One: Minu?

Missionary Mark: *(Throws hands up) Mi-nu*—who? Great day! I left my English-Ghanian dictionary in my luggage! English? Anyone here speak English?

(Another porter enters)

Porter Number Two: Sir, were you on Flight 219 from Atlanta?

Missionary Mark: Yes . . .

Porter Number Two: There was a slight mix-up in the luggage. All the bags marked West Africa accidentally went to West Germany and we are having some red tape problems. *(Missionary Mark groans)* But don't worry. They should be here in a few months. *(African music)*

Missionary Mark: Well, it's amazing how well this one outfit has lasted. Here comes dear Akumoah with the grub.

Akumoah: I brought you special delicacy! *(Foreign accent)*

Missionary Mark: Thanks Akumoah. I haven't had shish kebob in ages. *(Starts eating)* Mmmm . . . this steak is delicious!

Akumoah: Yes, me speared and cooked big fat rat just for missionary brother.

Missionary Mark: R-a-t! Excuse me—I feel slightly sick.

Akumoah: *(To audience)* Funny, white man not used to expensive delicacies!

(The following song can be sung by puppets to the tune of "Home Sweet Home")

(Song)

Despite culture shock,
And various rare foods,
The dedicated Mark,
Did very soon recoup.
From valleys low and mountain heights,
You can still see the glimmer of his (their) light(s).

Choir Ghosts

by Joan King

Sam, Bozart, Man, Bachtrovin, boy, Ghosts

Sam: *(Singing)* My grandfather's clock was too large for the shelf . . .

Bozart: Stop that noise! Stop those ridiculous sounds!

Sam: But, Mr. Bozart, I was just practicing my singing.

Bozart: Singing? Don't ever say that word in my shop again. You know better than to use seven-letter words like that around me. Singing—Bah Humbug!

Sam: But, Mr. Bozart, our choir is going to _____ next week, and I really need to condition my voice.

Bozart: Why would you need to condition your voice? What ever gave you the idea that I would ever let you off from work for a choir tour?

Sam: Well . . . I thought that . . . since I do have a solo . . . Maybe you might . . .

Bozart: Solo! You'll think "solo" by the time you finish all the work I'll give you. Music . . . choirs . . . tours . . . Bah. Humbug! *(Exits)*

Sam: Mr. Bozart will never let me go. The world will never get a chance to be exposed to the magnificent and thrilling voice of Sam Andervinski—never. Someone else will take my part while I stay in Mr. Bozart's shop and repair clocks. I wonder why Mr. Bozart hates music so?

(Man enters shop)

Man: Is Mr. Bozart in, Sam?

Bozart: Here I am. What do you want?

Man: Just a small donation to add happiness to a few lives, Mr. Bozart—a donation for our new choir robes.

Bozart: Choir robes? Never! I've just about had it with all of this talk about music. I hate music! I hate all music. Car horns, train whistles, birds in the trees singing tweet, tweet, tweet. I even get indigestion from having the dinner bell rung before I eat. Don't mention music to me. Get out of my shop and never come back again. *(They exit) (11:00 that night. Bozard in bed)*

Bachtrovin: Bozart, see this chain that I wear. I created this chain when we were partners in the clock repair business. We hated music together. We refused to work on musical clocks, chimes, and we even took the alarms out of clocks because of our hate for music. The tick tock with its perfect beat even drove us mad. My purpose for returning to the land of the living is to warn you of your fate if you continue as I did. You will bear this chain of sadness which grows heavier and heavier—without the joy that music gives to man when he praises God with his voice. Beware of this, Bozart, and let Sam Andervinski go on the choir tour next week.

Bozart: Bah! Humbug! I must have been dreaming.

Ghost I: Wolfgang Bozart.

Bozart: Who are you?

Ghost I: I am the ghost of choir past.

Bozart: What . . . do you want?

Ghost I: I have brought some memories along with me.

Remember when you were a little boy in choir and all of the other boys and girls were going on a tour? You didn't get to go, so you did some very mean things. First, you poured a whole gallon of cooking oil on the piano and Miss Melody, the pianist, slipped off the piano bench and broke her elbow. And then you gave the choir director a piece of bubble gum that had been soaked in green persimmon juice, and, to even be meaner, you glued all of the music together with the unused bubble gum. From that day forth you started hating music. That day began a lifetime of unhappiness. You can redeem yourself, however, by letting Sam go on his choir tour. Don't bear the guilt of bringing another music hater into the world.

Bozart: Come back. Tell me more.

Ghost II: Bozart.

Bozart: On no. Another one. What did I eat to make me have such nightmares?

Ghost II: You haven't eaten anything, Bozart. I am the Ghost of Choir Present. And I bring you warning also. You have been removing all of the alarms from the clocks of the choir members. You even take the radio out of clock radios so that no one can listen to Sunday night church services.

You must turn from your evil ways, Bozart, or you will never experience the joy of music.

Bozart: Am I dreaming or are those ghosts real? Music is not that important.

Ghost III: Oh, yes it is, Bozart. I am the Ghost of Choir Future. Look into the future with me and see how much sadness you are going to cause.

Little Boy: Wolfgang *(tin-eared)* Bozart. Nobody even came to the funeral. They say that old Mr. Bozart never sang a song all of his life. And that is what made him so grouchy. He wouldn't let my father go on choir tour. Now we never get to sing around our piano because Father is always so sad.

Bozart: I'll let him go, Little Sammy. I wouldn't want to bring that much unhappiness into the world.

(Singing heard in background.)

Bozart: Sam. Sam. I am here to tell everyone that I know that I have been wrong. Music is important. It can bring me happiness. I have decided to let you go on choir tour. And I am going to donate for choir robes. And I am going to join the choir!

The Choir Rehearsal

by Sarah Walton Miller

Mrs. Jay, Mrs. Oriole

Mrs. Jay: Oh, hello.

Mrs. Oriole: Hi. Are we ready to start rehearsal?

Mrs. Jay: Dreamer! Our director's not here yet.

Mrs. Oriole: Again? If all of us can get here on time, why not Mr. Nightingale?

Mrs. Jay: I know how you feel . . . Oh, look! There's Mr. Crow wearing another new suit.

Mrs. Oriole: He certainly is! I wonder how many he has?

Mrs. Jay: Really, I can't think why Mr. Nightingale tolerates him.

Mrs. Oriole: Well, for one thing—he's rich.

Mrs. Jay: But when he growls around on those low notes—

Mrs. Oriole: He claims he's singing bass!

Mrs. Jay: It sounds to me as if he has an upset stomach.

Mrs. Oriole: *(Turning)* Who's making all the fuss over there?

Mrs. Jay: It's Mr. Mockingbird pushing in to sit by Mr. Swallow.

Mrs. Oriole: Why?

Mrs. Jay: Mr. Mockingbord can't read a note!

Mrs. Oriole: *(Shocked)* Really?

Mrs. Jay: So he sits by Mr. Swallow and follows him.

Mrs. Oriole: If he can't read notes, why does Mr. Nightingale let him sing in the choir?

Mrs. Jay: Why does Mr. Nightingale do anything. Hasn't he let that woman dominate the alto section for years?

Mrs. Oriole: What woman?

Mrs. Jay: What woman? Why Clarabel Meadowlark!

Mrs. Oriole: Clarabel Meadowlark! Why, she's been in

the choir forever!

Mrs. Jay: Exactly. Of course she has. Do you know why?

Mrs. Oriole: Well, she does read music and she can sing —after a fashion. Not very pretty.

Mrs. Jay: Pish tush!

Mrs. Oriole: What do you mean—pish tush?

Mrs. Jay: She's been a member of the choir since the Year One because she gave the organ to the church forty years ago!

Mrs. Oriole: Oh, no!

Mrs. Jay: You didn't know that? Why, she's older than old Brother Owl—even if she does dress so young and spends all that money on her looks!

Mrs. Oriole: Well—she does sing on key.

Mrs. Jay: *(Annoyed)* That has nothing to do with it!

Mrs. Oriole: But I thought—

Mrs. Jay: Choir members should have the grace to retire by seventy-five, at least!

Mrs. Oriole: Oh, now! She's not seventy-five.

Mrs. Jay: Not far off. With a face-lift and some new clothes I could look pretty good, too.

Mrs. Oriole: *(Amused)* Has she really? A face-lift, I mean?

Mrs. Jay: Twice, I heard. Another one and her front will be around at her back!

Mrs. Oriole: Well, feature that! But even so, she doesn't sound any worse than a lot of others.

Mrs. Jay: And that's a recommendation? Quite confidentially—do you think Mr. Nightingale is the one for our choir?

Mrs. Oriole: Frankly no. For one thing, this always being late bugs me.

Mrs. Jay: Quite right. Oh, oh! Here he comes at last.

Both: *(Effusively)* Good evening, Mr. Nightingale!

Mrs. Oriole: . . . What did he say?

Mrs. Jay: He said, "Let's turn in the hymnal to 'Ready!' "

Mrs. Oriole: *(Disappointed)* That old thing?

Both: *(Singing)* Ready to go, ready to bear

Ready to watch and pray. *(Mrs. Oriole sings the last notes as an obbligato and goes flat. They stop suddenly)*

Mrs. Oriole: Now why did he stop us?

Mrs. Jay: *(Significantly)* Someone sang flat. In our section.

Mrs. Oriole: I didn't hear it.

Mrs. Jay: You wouldn't.

Mrs. Oriole: Oh? Just what did you mean by that?

Mrs. Jay: *(Kindly)* My dear—just think high. Then you'll have no trouble with those notes.

Mrs. Oriole: *(Miffed)* If there were wrong notes, I didn't sing them!

Mrs. Jay: *(Frostily)* Were you suggesting it was I?

Mrs. Oriole: If the shoe fits—

Mrs. Jay: There never was a day I couldn't sing circles around any soprano in this choir!

Mrs. Oriole: I never dreamed you could be so vindictive! Just because Mr. Nightingale gave me the solo in the anthem last Sunday!

Mrs. Jay: *(Maliciously)* Don't worry about it for a moment! No one could hear you, my dear! Tone projection is still one of your big problems, isn't it?

Mrs. Oriole: *(Angrily)* Let's sing!

Both: *(Sing as before)* Ready to go, ready to bear, Ready to watch and pray. Ready to stand aside and give

Till he shall clear the way. *(Mrs. Oriole again off)*

Mrs. Oriole: There! Mr. Nightingale ought to like that!

Mrs. Jay: If he's deaf.

Mrs. Oriole: What did you say?

Mrs. Jay: Nothing.

Mrs. Oriole: *(Surprised)* He's not letting us go already, is he?

Mrs. Jay: Looks like it. After all, it's the summer schedule.

Mrs. Oriole: Well—see you Sunday?

Mrs. Jay: Yes, indeed. And next Thursday, of course. I look forward to sitting with you at choir practice! *(They leave)*

Loneliness Is . . .

by Tommy Crow

Terry, Bill, Thomas

Bill: Tonight has really been a drag. Alice was busy, Jill's going out with Herbert, Mary's sick, and I don't have anything to do. I feel that nobody really cares about me; like nobody cares who I am or even if I'm alive.

Terry: You feel lonely Bill. Everybody feels lonely. When Jesus was on the cross, he was totally alone. He knew what loneliness was. However, through God's grace we are able to conquer our loneliness and reach out to others who are lonely.

Bill: What do you mean by "reach out to others who are lonely?"

Terry: There are all kinds of lonely people around. At school there are kids who don't have any friends at all. Then there are the people in the nursing homes all over the city that want someone to talk to. Why don't you come with me to one of the nursing homes and see what I'm talking about?

Bill: Well . . . OK.

(Thomas comes racing up in wheelchair)

Thomas: Did I hear someone say that they've come to visit me?

Terry: Hello Mr. Thomas, how are you doing?

Thomas: Fine considering . . . Who's your friend?

Terry: This is Bill. He's one of the young gentlemen from our church.

Bill: Hello.

Thomas: It's nice to see you. Kind of reminds me of my grandson. He should be starting to college about now. Of course I haven't seen him in a year, so I'm not sure if he made it or not.

Bill: When was the last time you saw your grandson?

Thomas: About a year, maybe's it's been two, I'm not sure. He's a big boy like you. Played football in junior high. I remember playing football with him before I got stuck in this wheelchair.

Terry: Mr. Thomas, do you ever feel lonely?

Thomas: Of course, everyone does, but I really do enjoy your visits.

Terry: Would you believe God has a promise for you?

Thomas: What is it?

Terry: God said that all of your friends who have already died will be waiting for you in heaven.

Thomas: We'll probably have a big reunion, and knowing those people up there, they'll serve angel food cake, and I love devil's food. *(Laughs)*

Terry: Be serious.

Thomas: OK. My . . . there goes one of the prettiest nurses we've got. I don't know when they started issuing that model. When I used to be in the hospital many years ago, the only nurses they had were four-by-four.

Bill: What did you do before you retired?

Thomas: I was the conductor of Number 17 of the Southern Pacific.

Bill: I've got a miniature of it in my train collection.

Thomas: Are you familiar with old 257? I worked on it when I first started.

Bill: Who doesn't? Would you mind if I adopted you?

Thomas: Of course it's OK.

Bill: I lost my grandfather when I was three, and I've never had a grandfather that I can remember. Why don't you tell me more about the railroads.

(Thomas and Bill exit, ad-libbing)

Terry: What you've just seen is something that might happen. All we are asking is that you get involved in another person's life for a short time each week or every other week in our nursing home ministry. We're not asking you to adopt someone like Bill did. We just want you to help in sharing God's love to a lot of lonely people.

Incident At Commencement*

by Tom deGaaf

Dean, Principal, Graduating Class

Dean: *(Enters wearing glasses and graduation-type hat)* Good evening Ladies and Gentlemen . . . and Graduating Class of '75 . . .
(He looks at the other end of stage—The Class of '75 isn't there—He gets very irritated)
I said Good evening Class of '75!

Class: *(They scramble into line at the other end of the stage—Bumping and banging into each other, muttering words of excitement and threats to each other)*

Dean: *(Annoyed. Clears his voice quite loudly for attention)* I said—Good evening Class of '75!

Class: *(Together—more or less)* Good evening Dean! *(One voice faintly is heard saying, "Good evening monster man")*

Dean: *(Turns his head quickly toward the Class to try and see who insulted him—Fails to see who it was)* All of your parents and friends are gathered here to see the Class of '75 graduate from high school . . . You all consider this a momentous occasion, and truly it is . . . You're excited to see them graduate and *(Glares at them)* I'm glad to see them go! . . . The dummies!

Principal: *(Enters dressed same as Dean—embarrassed at what the Dean just said—Tries to smooth things over)* Hee . . . Yes. We are proud of our students, aren't we Dean!

Dean: *(Looks over at the Class appraisingly)* . . . NO WAY!

Principal: *(Really flustered)* He was joking friends and parents, and School Board Members!

Dean: *(Stricken. Whispers to Principal)* . . . You didn't tell me the School Board Members would be here!

Principal: *(Whispers back)* . . . Well they are, and if you don't make an apology to them for insulting their graduating kids, you're going to get fired!

Dean: Oh excuse me folks! A thousand pardons . . . The principal just explained to me that you thought I was insulting this Class of '75 *(Points to them)* . . . NO, NO, NO . . . I was making reference to the Graduating Class of *(rival High School)!* I wouldn't dream of insulting our own *(Name)* High School students! No sireee! They're the finest bunch of scholars in the country!

Principal: *(Whispers to Dean)* . . . What you said was terrific! I think the School Board and parents fell for it!

Dean: I think I'm going to be sick!

Principal: Now Ladies and Gentlemen, the time you have waited for is here!—The Graduation Ceremony!
(Class members straighten up their lines and stand at attention, each waiting for his name to be called) (Make a list of all the graduating students that will be at the banquet. Select a funny award to give each person as his representative puppet walks across the stage to graduate. Example: —Most athletic—Most likely to succeed—Most likely Not to succeed—Best Smile—Weirdest—Most likely to become a Zoo Sweeper, and so forth.

Puppets march across the stage as award is being announced. Each puppet shakes hands with Principal and Dean. Then exits behind the stage. Puppet re-enters at the end of the line again to portray another person. Puppets "Whoop" for joy each time they shake hands and exit)

Principal: Well Ladies and Gentlemen, Parents and School Board members, that concludes the Commencement Exercises for 1975!

Dean: *(Whispers to Principal)* Don't you think we ought to warn 'em about the empty diplomas some of those little meatheads got?

Principal: *(Whispers back)* I changed my mind and decided to pass All of 'em.

Dean: *(Shocked)* You mean you even passed (several kid's names)?

Principal: It was either that or have to put up with 'em for one more year!

Dean: Good thinkin'!! Yep!! Good thinkin'!! Now let's split it on over to Mrs. Honeyhurt's place for the party! You even passed that dummy *(Graduate's name)??* *(They exit together)*

Section V
FUN AND FELLOWSHIP

The First Ski Boat— Also the Slowest*

by Tom deGraaf

Willie, Cool Charlie, Rita Strumph

Willie: *(He and Cool Charlie enter. Both have beach towels around neck. Cool Charlie has on sunglasses)* I sure wish we could go waterskiing!

Charlie: You said it man! I've been sittin' around the house for hours tryin' to think of a way to single ski my bathtub!

Willie: We gotta find somebody with a boat! I mean that's all there is to it! You just can't do your best waterskiing without a boat. I mean I've tried too. Yesterday I got Sally to tow me behind her tricycle across our neighbor's wet lawn and all I did was bust the fin off my ski! Then Dad busted a fin off me when he saw the rut job I put on that lawn!

Charlie: How are we going to get a ski boat?

Rita: *(Offstage)* Oh Willieee—Cool Charlieee—Where are you?

Charlie: Oh no! It's that clunky Rita Strumph from our Sunday School class.

Willie: You mean the one who knows every story there is in the Bible and makes us listen to her tell 'em all the time?

Charlie: The same.

Willie: Oh no! How are we ever going to get rid of her? We'll never go skiing once she starts in on us with one of her stories and she loves to tell them just so—with every detail exactly correct. I mean who cares if David smacked Goliath with a smooth stone or a brick? He got him didn't he?

Charlie: That's it! When Rita comes up to bug us, I'll start telling her a story, only I'll change a few things. That'll drive her crazy and she'll just get mad and leave!

Willie: Great idea! Uh oh—Here she comes. Rita

Strumph—Kook!

Rita: *(Enters)* Hi boys! I see you're both dressed up like . . . *(Thinks)* . . . like shepherds! That reminds me of the story of Jacob and his brothers who . . .

Willie: *(Interrupts)* Hi Rita—How's everything going for you?

Rita: Going for me? That reminds me of the story of Philip going down the road with the Eunuch. It seems they were . . .

Charlie: *(Interrupts)* Hi Rita baby! How are you doing?

Rita: Baby? That reminds me of the story about the baby Moses who was put in a river by his sister because . . .

Charlie: *(Interrupts)* River? Hey Rita that reminds me of a story! *(He and Willie look at each other and give the "thumbs-up" sign.)*

Rita: *(Shocked)* You know a story? I didn't think you knew anything but a limited amount of trivia.

Charlie: *(To Willie)* What'd she say? *(Willie shrugs.)* Well anyway, I happen to know the story about the first and also the slowest ski boat in history! *(Proudly)* Right Willie? *(Willie nods.)*

Rita: That's a Bible story?

Willie: What's a matter with you Rita? Haven't you ever heard of Noah's Arch?

Charlie: Ark, Idiot!

Rita: Why certainly I do! Furthermore, I can tell that story perfectly. Down to the last detail. It was made of gopher wood you know.

Willie: Noah?

Rita: The arch—uh ark, silly! Cool Charlie, you may begin the story. There are only two things in life that make me happy: One is hearing me tell a Bible story, and the other is hearing someone else tell a Bible story—providing it's done well and correctly. You may begin.

Charlie: Thank you Toots. Here's the story. *(Looks at Willie. They give the "thumbs-up")* Once upon a time there was a guy named Noah Arch who lived in California and rented out water-ski boats.

Rita: *(Gasps in horror)* Aaarrrggghhph!!! That ain't it at all!!! That's no where even close to the story! Noah's last name was not Arch! He did not live in California and he did not rent ski boats! Now you tell it right, Cool Charlie!!!

Willie: Are you getting upset?

Rita: Yes! Very!

Charlie: *(He and Willie give "thumbs-up")* OK—OK Rita. I'll tell it right. So one day God noticed that some of Noah's customers were cheatin' on him—Swipin' engine parts and stuff. So he told Noah that he was going to send a hurricane, a typhoon, a tidal wave, plus a Lawnboy sprinkler to drown everyone on the earth for being bad!

Rita: *(Out of control—Frantic)* Aaaarrrggggphphssss!! I told you to tell this story right Cool Charlie and I meant it! What you said is not true at all. Noah lived a long time ago and God said because the people were sinful he was going to send a flood to destroy them.

Charlie: That's what I meant. So Noah started building the biggest ski boat in the world. And just before the flood came, he loaded his family, his dog, and a pair of rabbits into the boat, cranked her up, and headed off for Catalina.

Rita: *(Bananas)* Yeeeeeekkkaarrgghuph!! That does it Cool Charlie!

Charlie: *(Innocently)* Something wrong?

Rita: You have completely ruined the story! Noah built an ark, not a ski boat. He took two or more of all the animals in the world, not just his dog and a pair of rabbits. Furthermore, I am so disgusted with you and Willie that I'm leaving!

Charlie: Good!

Rita: Don't beg me to stay! I said I'm leaving and that's final.

Willie: At least now we can go find us a water-ski boat. *(He and Charlie give the "thumbs-up"—mission accomplished.)*

Rita: Did you say ski boat?

Charlie: Yes. Bye.

Rita: Well! My dad just brought a new ski boat and is using it today, but I'm certainly not going to invite you two to come along. *(She exits.)*

Willie: *(He and Charlie look at each other in shocked silence.)* We really blew it this time.

Charlie: You and your silly ideas about Noah's arch . . . I'm sick.

Willie: I guess we got just what we deserved—Just like those guys who missed the boat Noah was runnin'!

Rita: *(Offstage)* . . . Aw come on you guys—I'll give you one more chance—Let's go skiing!

Charlie: *(Excited)* Another chance! We lucked out.

Rita: *(From below)* Are you guys comin' or should I take some rabbits?

Boys: Yaaaaahooo! We're coming'. *(They exit whooping it up.)*

Incident at the Dentist's Office*

by Tom deGraaf

Willie, Dentist, Nurse

Willie: *(Enters with handkerchief around head and jaws—moaning)* Oooohh, Ouch! This toothache is killing me! If I don't see the dentist soon I think I'll go into shock —or possibly glossolalia!

Nurse: *(Flighty)* La-la-a-bop-e-dop! Oh, hi there sick person! You gotta toothache or did your head come gift-wrapped? Haw Haw Haw!

Willie: *(Looks sourly at the audience. Then back at Nurse)* I have a bad toothache and I would like to see the dentist if you don't mind!

Nurse: That's fine with me rabbit face. *(She pulls at the two ends of the handkerchief on top of Willie's head)* We get all kinds in here. Last week this weird hippie came in and said he wanted a tooth transplant from his Doberman!

Willie: *(Shocked)* A tooth transplant from a Doberman? What for?

Nurse: I don't know. Once we got 'em in, We didn't have the nerve to ask him! That Kook bit everybody in the waiting room and ruined all the tires in the parking lot. Besides that, I don't think he's gonna pay his bill!!

Willie: Let me outa here! *(Starts to leave. Nurse grabs him by the handkerchief "ears")* You guys are all crazy!

Nurse: Hey, You haven't seen the dentist yet! *(Struggles with Willie)* You'll like him. He watches "Night Stalker" a lot!

Dentist: *(Enters. Kind of crazy)* Hel-lo there sick person! Got a toothache? *(Looks at handkerchief "ears")* . . . or are you Patty Hearst disguised as Bugs Bunny? The Flying Nun?

Willie: *(Stops fighting with Nurse)* I am a normal person with a typical toothache! Now will you help me or not!?!

Nurse: Ain't he cute? Let's operate!

Dentist: OK buddy, open yer mouth so I can have a look-see at your chompers. And don't breathe on me either beetlebreath!

Willie: *(To Nurse)* That's a doctor? I've heard better medical terminology on the soap operas! *(Opens mouth)* Aaahhh . . .

Dentist: *(He and Nurse peer in)* Hmmmm . . . Yuk-O! What in the world?

Nurse: *(Still looking)* That's the strangest thing I've ever seen! Somebody tied his uvula in a knot!

Willie: That happened last week during choir practice. Now will you get with it!

Dentist: It's going to have to come out!

Nurse: His mouth?

Dentist: No, Madame Curie, that big chunk of *tinfoil* he's got stuck between his teeth. *(Both look into Willie's mouth)*

Willie: You mean it's not really a rotten tooth?

Nurse: *(Fanning)* Rotten breath maybe. Rotten tooth, no. How could anybody be so stupid as to put a big chunk of tinfoil in his mouth?

Dentist: What'd ya do? Eat a TV dinner whole? *(Both Nurse and Dentist break into hysterical laughter)* Haw Haw Haw!

Nurse: Maybe he ate a complete Jiffy-Pop popcorn thing! *(Laughs)*

Willie: *(Looks at them both disgustedly)* That's what I get for eating at a church potluck! *(Sulks off)*

Hee Haw Fling

by Carroll Bryant Brown

Announcer, Judd, Minnie, Odel, Ernie

(TV Announcer enters to music. As music stops suddenly . . .)

TV Announcer: This here program is brought to you by the makers of Crunchy Kangaroo Cereal. The cereal with 30 percent iron, 20 percent phosphorus, 8 percent zinc, and 6 percent natural vitamins. It doesn't snap, crackle, or pop. It just stays there and rusts. *(Music interlude. Sign says, "Hee, Haw!" Judd and Minnie enter)*

Judd: Minnie, when you were younger, you used to nibble on my ear! *(Minnie starts to leave)* Hey, where are you going?

Minnie: To get my teeth! *(Pause for laugh)*

Minnie: When I went out with Oscar, I had to slap his face five times.

Judd: Why, Minnie! Was he that fresh? Just wait till I get my hands on him!

Minnie: No . . . I thought he was dead! *(Exit. Music and sign interlude. Odel and Ernie enter)*

Odel: Ernie, dear, I just came from the beauty parlor.

Ernie: You did? What happened? Was it closed? *(Odel hits him on the head)*

Ernie: You know *(Someone familiar)*'s family must really be poor.

Odel: Why?

Ernie: Well, everytime he walks down the street, people are always saying, "There goes _____ . I pity his poor family." *(Exit. Let out a horselaugh and screaming giggle. Music interlude)*

TV Announcer: And now for the weather report. Today sunny, followed by muggy, Tuggy, Wenggy, Thurgy, and Friggy. *(Music interlude. Judd and Minnie enter. Music stops)*

Judd: Minnie, what would I have to give you for one little kiss on the cheek?

Minnie: A bottle of poison!

Judd: Minnie, you are simply driving me out of my mind.

Minnie: That's not a drive . . . that's a putt!

Minnie: Aren't you proud of me, Judd? I lost ten pounds!

Judd: Turn around, Minnie. I think I found them. *(Loud laugh as Minnie hits him)*

Judd: Uhm . . . I wish I had a nickel for every girl I'd kissed.

Minnie: You'd be as broke as a church mouse. *(Exit. Music and sign interlude. Odel and Ernie enter)*

Ernie: When I look at Kentucky Fried Chicken, I want a leg . . . but when I look at you, I want to neck!

Odel: *(Grasps and hits Ernie)*

Ernie: Odel, does your dad mind an idiot around the house?

Odel: I don't guess so . . . you come right often! *(Pause for laugh)*

Ernie: Now, Odel, you know I'm one of the smartest, best-looking fellows in school.

Odel: Why did you get a zero on your spelling test then?

Ernie: The teacher ran out of stars, so she gave me a moon! *(Exit. Music and sign interlude)*

TV Announcer: At this time daily, we pause to recognize our "Lady for the Day." Today we have a young lady who represents one of the fastest growing, most popular groups in many of our homes . . . Let's hear it for Miss Rhoda

Roach! *(Applause. Music interlude Judd and Minnie enter. Minnie has a menu in her hand)*

Minnie: Gee, Judd, there isn't any soup on the menu.

Judd: Of course not, Minnie. They run a clean joint here.

Minnie: I think I'll have a hard boiled egg!

Judd: Well, that's something hard to beat! *(Lets out a horse laugh)* I think I'll just get a tutti frutti.

Minnie: What in tarnation is that?

Judd: A pineapple playing a trumpet! *(Music, interlude Odel and Minnie enter for some girl chat)*

Odel: Have you tried any new recipes, Minnie?

Minnie: Well, I crossed a ghost with evaporated milk.

Odel: What did you get?

Minnie: Nothing. *(Lets out a screaming giggle)*

Odel: Well, I baked two kinds of biscuits today. Would you like to take your pick?

Minnie: No thank you. I'll use my hammer! *(Pause for laugh)*

Odel: Oh, by the way, Minnie, do you want your coffee black?

Minnie: What other colors do you have? *(Music and Sign interlude)*

TV Announcer: And now to conclude our show—We have two scientific minds at "Battle of Wits."

Judd: *(Singing)* You load sixteen tons and what do you get?

Ernie: A hernia!

Judd: Ernie, did you know that a grasshopper on the moon could jump a hundred times its length?

Ernie: Nope. But here on earth, I saw a wasp lift a two-hundred-pound man three feet off the ground!

Judd: Ernie, which travels faster—heat or cold?

Ernie: Ah shucks Judd, that's easy. Heat of course. You can catch cold.

Ernie: Judd, what do you feed a five-hundred-pound kitty cat?

Judd: Anything he wants. Just anything he wants.

Judd: Tell me something important about the scientists of the eighteenth century.

Ernie: They're all dead! *(Horse laugh—music and interlude)*

TV Announcer: Well folks, until next week's show, keep smiling. This last portion of our program has been brought to you by Beautyrest Pillows—the five-year deodorant pads guaranteed to stop perspiration. *(Music)*

"Miss Churchie" Pageant

by Carroll Bryant Brown

Narrator, M. C., Miss Sunday Schoolie, Miss Churchie Training, Miss Missions, Miss Wreck-reation, Miss Vocal Chords, Miss Back-slider

Narrator: Welcome to the First International Pageant of Miss Churchie. Contestants for our pageant tonight come to us from around the world. Each contestant is judged on beauty, talent, and originality. All week these contestants have been competing in rounds—tonight alive from _____ (insert name of church) in _____ (town), we bring you the final round on "originality." And now from Bible Belt, U.S.A.—our famous Mr. M. C.

M. C.: *(Runs out, amid clapping and shouting. Bows)* Thank you. *(As the audience quietens, he begins singing, "Miss Churchie")*
Miss Church-ie—here she comes, She's Number One in the Land.

She's the top!
She's the best!
She's just one of a kind and
Here she comes now—
Our Gal—Church-ie. *(Applauding and bowing)*
And now, ladies and gentlemen—are you ready? Could we have the question from the judges? *(Judge brings a white envelope to M. C. He opens and reads)* The question is "Why do you think that you should get 'Miss Churchie Woman'?" And now for our first contestant—Miss Sunday Schoolie. *(She enters to music of "Holy Bible, Book Divine")*
Now could you tell us in thirty words or less "Why do you

think you should be 'Miss Churchie Woman'?''

Miss Sunday Schoolie: *(Gets louder as she talks)* I think I should win because of the importance of learning the Scriptures and what they mean to us. *(Raises voice)* For, man does not live by bread alone, but by every word that cometh out of the mouth. The time of judgement is at hand . . . repent . . . *(Exits still preaching)*

M.C.: Whew! Talk about woman's ordination! And now, Miss Churchie Training. What a gal! *(Audience whistles)* OK! You know the question—do your thing!

Miss Churchie Training: *(Gets serious after whistling)* We are making an effort to develop our total selves as women and churchmakers. I think I should win because of my versatility. Any area you're lacking in—that's my bag. Anyone with as many talents as me should, of course, be the winner! *(Exits with confidence)*

M.C.: Talk about conceit! And now for the next cookie—Miss Wreck-reation. *(She enters to cheering or march record)*

Miss Wreck-reation: Howdy, gang. Let's go! Let's go! Wreck-reaction is my one gal show! Ha, Ha!

M.C.: *(Gasps)* Lively number. Well, dearie, why do you feel that you should be ''Miss Churchie''?

Miss Wreck-reation: The Bible says our bodies are the temples of God. My job is to loosen up, tighten up, and shape up—all the sags, bags, and hags. Ha! I think I should win because after all, *(Begins philosophying)*, what is life without sunshine, laughter, and fun? *(Exits doing a cheer)*

Give me a W	Give me a R
Give me a R	Give me a E
Give me a E	Give me a A
Give me a C	Give me a T
Give me a K	Give me a I
	Give me a O
	Give me a N

What you got? A winner! *(Exits)*

M.C.: With spirit like that—who needs vitamins? And the next contestant—Miss Missions. Dig her rig!

Miss Missions: *(Enters to Oriental music)* Africa, Brazil, Israel, Philippines, Korea—you name it, and I'm there and interested. I think that I should be ''Miss Churchie Woman'' because I have friends the world over who believe that I am important and who are supporting me. And after all, if you have friends the world over, how can you lose?

M. C.: How, indeed! And now Miss Vocal Chords.

Miss Vocal Chords: *(Enters Singing)* Do, Re, Mi, Fa, Sol, La, Ti, *Do (Breaks glass on last note)*

M. C.: Ugh, yes, very shattering, and now please answer your question.

Miss Vocal Chords: I bring joy, Sunshine, and music into your life. What is life without song? It's quite evident that I should be ''Miss Churchie Woman.'' Just let your ears be the judge.

Glory, Halleluia, Glory, Halleluia . . . *(Exits as M. C. covers his ears)*

M. C.: Well, it's time for the judges' final decision. Will the judges please present the winner? *(Drum rolls as judge hands M. C. the envelope)*

M. C.: The winner of our First International ''Miss Churchie'' Pageant is *(Gasps)* ugh, Miss Back-slider. *(She enters as music plays.)*

Miss Back-slider: Busy, busy me
With parties, school, and tea.
I'd like to get involved,
And have some of my problems solved.
Church is fine when you have the time.
But not for a busy lady like me!
(M. C. starts singing ''Here She Comes, Miss Churchie.'' Judges crown her and give her flowers and robe)

M. C.: Until next year . . . *(Throws kiss)*

Valentine Songs . . .*

1. "Ain't No Mountain High Enough"—A *Record* by the Supremes

   A Female lead singer, Two Female backup singers

   If possible, use black puppets for most natural setting. Use two microphones put on stands side-by-side for the backup singers, and let the lead singer puppet hold hers. As the music begins, have the puppets gracefully 'jive' up to their respective mikes in some style of black choreography—with group coordinated hand jives and body movements. Ad-lib choreography but the backup singers always do exactly the same moves.

2. "It Hurts So Bad"—A *Record* by The Lettermen

   Four male singers with matching costumes

   Puppets sing in pairs around two mike stands. Stylize choreography with dramatic pauses and head turns. Follow what the words say to do.

3. "Mr. Postman"—*Record* by the Carpenters

   A flustered female, A backup trio

   A harried postman complete with uniform and mailbag Backup trio is grouped around a mike (on a stand). They do the backup singing parts, plus the saxophone and guitar solos. They appear to be in a world of their own, completely oblivious to the action going around them. They do every-thing the same way except on the sax and guitar solos. Then as one does the solo, the other two turn and watch him and jive. The lead female singer is your typical man-starved female who wants the postman to bring her a letter from her boyfriend (whether the mailman has a letter or not). She sings through the first verse of the record to establish her plight. From then on she chases the mailman each time he appears, (during the instrumental solos). Each time he eludes her and disappears. She stops and looks around dismally wondering where he could have gone, and continues to sing. Finally as the end of the song nears and the music fades, the mailman appears (with his mailbag) again, and she chases him around and then down behind the curtain again. Then the audience hears him yelp and sees a big pile of letters go flying into the air. As the music almost quits, she emerges excitedly waving a letter! The mailman staggers up (quite beat up looking), glances at her, shakes his head and passes out, falling backwards. The backup group nonchalantly walks down behind the curtain as the female waves bye to the audience with her letter and follows down. (Note: On the sax solo, have a toy sax that one of the backup can grab in his mouth. On guitar solo, have an extra person hold up a real guitar and let a backup flail away at it like he's playing it.)

*Adapted from *California Puppets*, Mill Valley, California. © Copyright, 1975. Used by permission.

A Patriotic Musical*

by Tom deGraaf

Paul Johnson's—"Spirit of '76" (Tempo Records)

Select five or six songs that are usable with your puppets. Put the songs on tape. Next, build a stage in three sections. Work out your own choreography and then present the musical by itself or in conjunction with your Youth Choir. If done with the Youth Choir, mix up the actual singing and the taped voices. Let the puppets sing a few songs and the choir sing a few!

*Reprinted from *California Puppets*, Mill Valley, California. © Copyright, 1975. Used by permission.